Ezra & Nehemiah

60 Daily Insights by **Robert M. Solomon**

Journey Through Ezra & Nehemiah
© 2020 by Robert M. Solomon
All rights reserved.

Our Daily Bread Publishing is affiliated
with Our Daily Bread Ministries.

Requests for permission to quote
from this book should be directed to:
Permissions Department
Our Daily Bread Publishing
P.O. Box 3566
Grand Rapids, MI 49501
Or contact us by email at
permissionsdept@dhp.org

Design by Joshua Tan
Typeset by Lidya Jap

ISBN 978-1-913135-27-0

Printed in the United Kingdom
Second Printing in 2020

Foreword

As we read the ancient history recorded in the books of Ezra and Nehemiah, we may ask: What does it have to do with modern life? What lessons can there be for us today?

The answer is: God's Word is fresh for every generation! Even today, Ezra-Nehemiah continues to educate and inspire us on what is important for God's people.

Three central themes can be found in these two books: the priority of worship, the centrality of the Word, and the necessity of witnessing to the world by obeying God. Both Ezra and Nehemiah emphasise worship and the Word, while Nehemiah also stresses the importance of maintaining walls and gates. It is a timely reminder for us today to be holy and separate from the sinful world, while still being effective witnesses to it.

Come, let us meditate on Ezra-Nehemiah. For it is in these two books that we will find a deeper understanding of God and His ways, and draw inspiration from how He relates to His people and how He fulfils His promises. May God continue to speak to us through His enduring Word and work out His will in our lives!

Robert M. Solomon

We're glad you've decided to join us on a journey into a deeper relationship with Jesus Christ!

For over 50 years, we have been known for our daily Bible reading notes, *Our Daily Bread*. Many readers enjoy the pithy, inspiring, and relevant articles that point them to God and the wisdom and promises of His unchanging Word.

Building on the foundation of *Our Daily Bread*, we have developed this devotional series to help believers spend time with God in His Word, book by book. We trust this daily meditation on God's Word will draw you into a closer relationship with Him through our Lord and Saviour, Jesus Christ.

How to use this resource

READ: This book is designed to be read alongside God's Word as you journey with Him. It offers explanatory notes to help you understand the Scriptures in fresh ways.

REFLECT: The questions are designed to help you respond to God and His Word, letting Him change you from the inside out.

RECORD: The space provided allows you to keep a diary of your journey as you record your thoughts and jot down your responses.

An Overview

The Old Testament books of Ezra and Nehemiah were considered one book in ancient times. They were possibly the work of a single author, and often seen as a continuation of 1 & 2 Chronicles. It is mainly a historical narrative covering Israel's history from 538 BC to 433 BC.

The story brings us back to the period of Jewish exile in Babylon, when a decree of the Persian emperor Cyrus in 538 BC led to the return of 50,000 Jews to Jerusalem. (Jerusalem had been destroyed in 586 BC by Babylonian king Nebuchadnezzar.) God had not forgotten His people, and had brought them back to their holy city. The books have sections written in the first person "I", reflecting contributions from Ezra and Nehemiah.

Ezra-Nehemiah covers three successive missions to rebuild Jerusalem. Ezra 1–6 deals with the first group of returnees, who rebuilt the temple under the leadership of Zerubbabel and the spiritual guidance of the prophets Haggai and Zechariah. Ezra 7–10 deals with the second group of returnees, who were led by the scribe Ezra in 458 BC and whose mission it was to teach the law and encourage the people to keep it faithfully. Nehemiah 1–6 records the rebuilding of the city walls under Nehemiah's leadership in 445 BC, while Nehemiah 7–13 tells the story of the renewal of the covenant and some lingering problems in the community that Nehemiah had to deal with.

Structure of Ezra and Nehemiah

Ezra 1–6	The first return and rebuilding of the temple
Ezra 7–10	Ezra's mission to teach and establish the law
Nehemiah 1–6	Nehemiah leads in rebuilding the wall of Jerusalem
Nehemiah 7–13	Building the covenantal community

Key Verse

Because the hand of the LORD my God was on me, I took courage and gathered leaders from Israel to go up with me. —Ezra 7:28

Day 1

Read Ezra 1:1–4

Have you ever felt as if God has forgotten you? Perhaps you have been stuck in an unhappy situation for a long time, and your prayers to God remain unanswered.

The Jews must have felt this way when they were exiled to Babylon after Jerusalem was destroyed in 586 BC. Many were homesick and wondered whether they would ever see their beloved city of Jerusalem again. They sang, "By the rivers of Babylon we sat and wept when we remembered Zion" (Psalm 137:1). Those who were familiar with the message of the prophets knew God had promised that after a 70-year period of captivity, He would bring the captives back to Jerusalem (Jeremiah 25:8–11; 29:10). In fact, before this period was up, God was already at work, as if eager to fulfil His promise.

God "moved the heart" (Ezra 1:1) of Cyrus, the Persian king who had overthrown the Babylonian empire. Who would have thought that God would be at work in the king's heart? Through the prophet Isaiah, God had already foretold, some 150 years before, how He would use Cyrus to do His will (Isaiah 44:28–45:5).

So the unthinkable happens. The pagan king issues an edict freeing the Jewish exiles to return to Jerusalem to rebuild the temple (Ezra 1:2–4). He also attributes his rise to power to "The LORD, the God of heaven" and sees his mission as helping to build a temple for God in the holy city (v. 2).

A relatively small group of 50,000 Jews return home—a remnant, as God had foretold (Isaiah 10:22). In Jerusalem itself, a small group of "survivors" remain. They are poor and have suffered badly (see Jeremiah 40:7; Lamentations 5:2–5, 11–13). Cyrus orders that these people be assisted with money and resources to rebuild the temple (Ezra 1:4).

It is an amazing turning point in the history of the Jews. **When all seems lost, God turns a new page with His sovereign hand, demonstrating that He remembers—and will fulfil—His promises.** This can encourage us today, especially if we feel that God has forgotten us and His promises. If we wait for Him with faith, He will never disappoint.

Recall a situation in your life when you may have felt helpless. How did your situation change, and what did you learn about God and His promises?

God mentioned Cyrus by name 150 years before he was born, and later used him to help His people. What confidence does this give you? How can you apply such knowledge of God in your life?

Day 2

Read Ezra 1:5–6

Have you ever faced a task that is so difficult and overwhelming that you start to wonder: Should you do it in the first place? In such circumstances, what is the key factor that would keep us going?

In the book of Ezra, the Jews face a task that seems to have insurmountable odds. Rebuild a temple in a city that has laid in waste for more than 50 years? Impossible! God knows the difficulty of the task, however, and He provides the key factor that will keep them going— He moves their hearts. God moves the heart of Cyrus, the hearts of the leaders of the Jewish exiles in Babylon, and the hearts of the Jews themselves.

The heart must be moved first before the feet follow suit. **God's work in our hearts is vital if we are to start and complete what He wills for us to do.** The ESV Bible uses the phrase, "whose spirit God had stirred" (Ezra 1:5), showing that the moving of one's heart is a deep work of God himself. He is the One "who works in you to will and to act in order to fulfil his good purpose" (Philippians 2:13). Without this movement of the Holy Spirit within us, our actions will lack spiritual life and power. Only when the call of God is clear, are we able to do God's will no matter how difficult the circumstances and no matter the setbacks and disappointments.

Not all the Jews make the move, only those whose spirits are stirred by God. Every person whose heart is moved by God joins those who return to Jerusalem on their holy mission. The gifts and freewill offerings given to the returning exiles are signs that God is with them (Ezra 1:6).

The same thing happened when God led His people out of slavery in Egypt under the leadership of Moses. As the Israelites were leaving, God made the Egyptians favourably disposed when they were asked for gold, silver, and clothing for the journey (Exodus 12:35–36). The unusual response of the Egyptians must have been an encouragement to the departing Israelites as they stepped into an unknown future.

God has His way of working in us and encouraging us on the way. Perhaps you sense God stirring something in your heart now. You feel a divine nudge to go somewhere, to do something, or to embark on a new journey. Prayerfully trust God and do His bidding. He will encourage you by providing what is needed, which is a way of saying that He is with you. "The one who calls you is faithful, and he will do it" (1 Thessalonians 5:24).

ThinkThrough

Read Acts 8:21. Why has an untouched heart no part in serving God? How can we ensure that our hearts are not far from God? Consider how God may be moving your heart in a certain direction.

What is the difference between a heart that is moved by God and superficial enthusiasm created by human means? Which is preferred in our individual lives and in our local churches? Pray accordingly.

Day 3

Read Ezra 1:7–11

A person loses his luggage at a busy airport, makes a report of his loss, and leaves the airport feeling sad. A few days later, the airport calls him to tell him his bag has been found. He retrieves the bag and finds that all his belongings are intact. What a relief!

Unfortunately, the Jews will not experience a similar sentiment upon their return to Jerusalem. Nothing is left intact in Jerusalem. Not only has the temple been destroyed by the Babylonians in 586 BC, but all the valuable articles inside it have also been taken away by the conquerors (2 Chronicles 36:18). These articles were made during the Exodus by Spirit-enabled craftsmen according to God's instructions (Exodus 31:1–10), and were used for the worship of God.

The Israelites have lost so much of their worship of God because of their disobedience. The temple is no more, and the temple articles are now in a pagan Babylonian temple (Ezra 1:7). Without the temple and the articles needed to worship God, the Israelites are not able to worship Him with the right rituals as prescribed by the law of Moses.

But God is at work. When He restores, He goes all the way. Not only does Cyrus permit the Jews to return to Jerusalem to rebuild the temple, but he also orders all the articles that were seized from the original temple to be returned to the Jews (v. 7). An empty temple without its furnishings and articles would not have been of much use for the ritual worship required of Israel.

The Persian treasurer makes a careful list of the 5,400 articles and hands them over to Sheshbazzar, the governor of Judah (vv. 8–11). Many scholars think that the names Sheshbazzar (meaning "joy in affliction") and Zerubbabel ("a stranger in Babylon") actually belong to the same person who led the Jews back to Jerusalem. Missing in the list, however, are the key furnishings in the temple, such as the altars, golden lampstand, and ark of the covenant, which had probably been lost. Note, for instance, that a new altar had to be built (3:1–6).

Sheshbazzar leads the exiles "from Babylon to Jerusalem" (1:11). **God has kept His promise and is bringing a remnant of His people back to Jerusalem so that His temple can be rebuilt and His people can worship Him there.** The Lord is a master at restoration. It is He who said, "I will repay you for the years the locusts have eaten" (Joel 2:25), and it is He who blessed Job twice as much as he had before being afflicted (Job 42:10). Whatever we may lose by straying from God, He is able to restore when we return to Him.

Do you think there is something that you or your church have lost in worship? If so, how can it be restored?

"From Babylon to Jerusalem" (Ezra 1:11) represents a momentous turning point. What does it mean personally for you?

Day 4

Read Ezra 2:1–58

Today's reading contains a detailed list of the people who return to Jerusalem. There are 49,897 people and 8,136 animals (Ezra 2:64–67). We may wonder why the Bible has such details. God has His reasons for including them; in this case, they teach us some truths. Let me highlight three.

Firstly, the list shows us that God has preserved the key leadership of the nation. Eleven names are recorded in the leadership group (Ezra 2:2); the parallel passage Nehemiah 7:7 lists twelve. **Though the returnees are only a remnant, the twelve leaders represent the full Israelite community.** (The Nehemiah and Mordecai mentioned in Ezra 2:2 are not the famous figures in the books of Nehemiah and Esther.) Zerubbabel is a royal descendant of David, and his fellow leader, Joshua, is a high priest (Zechariah 3:1).

Secondly, the list shows us that God extends His grace not only to Israel but also to those outside Israel. The returnees are numbered according to their families and their vocation in the temple services. Only the men are numbered, meaning that the total number of people was more. The priests mentioned (Ezra 2:36–39) make up only four of the 24 divisions established by King David

(1 Chronicles 24:1–19). This means that the majority of priests in exile had chosen to remain in Babylon. As for the Levites, even fewer choose to return (Ezra 2:40). The fact that there was a greater pool of Levites than priests—who were descended from only one of Levi's several descendants—makes the poor response from the Levites even more significant.

Thankfully, there are also some musicians and gatekeepers (vv. 41–42) who return to Jerusalem to serve there. Two other groups are mentioned: the temple servants (vv. 43–54) and the descendants of the servants of Solomon (vv. 55–57). The former group (*Nethinim* in Hebrew) probably refers to the Gibeonites who had deceived the Israelites in the days of Joshua but were put into service as temple servants (Joshua 9). The latter group was probably made up of descendants of foreigners employed by King Solomon (2 Chronicles 8:7–8). God extended His grace to those outside Israel.

Thirdly, God knows each of His children and has their names written in the Book of Life. The individual names show the influence of Israelite theology as well as Babylonian and Persian culture. Some of the names are very personal and even funny: Ater (Ezra 2:16) means "lefty", Hashum (v. 19) means "broad nose", and Gibbar (v. 20) means "strong man".

The list reminds us of God's Book of Life (Revelation 3:5), and how each person is known by God and precious to Him. Those who are saved in Christ will have their names permanently in this book. It is good to remember God's faithfulness in keeping His promises, and His grace that is extended to us in a personal way. These are reasons to worship Him with trust and gratitude.

Why are name lists important to God? Why is having your name in God's Book of Life so vital, and how does one get into that list? How certain are you that God knows you personally?

Most of the priests and Levites stayed in their comfort zones and refused to be involved in the great work that God was doing. How can you avoid doing the same?

Read Ezra 2:59–63

A family flee their war-torn nation and take a raft across the Mediterranean Sea towards safer shores. The raft sinks, but fortunately the family is rescued. However, as they have lost their identity papers, it is very difficult for them to persuade the authorities that they are genuine refugees.

Some in the group of returnees to Jerusalem face a similar difficulty. They claim to be from priestly lines, but cannot prove it (Ezra 2:61–62). Priests in Israel had to be certified by virtue of their pedigree: God had chosen the tribe of Levi to serve Him in the temple, and from them, the descendants of Aaron to be priests (Numbers 18:5–7). Some 600 years earlier, in the time of the judges, a Jew called Micah had built a religious shrine and appointed his son—and subsequently, a Levite outside the priestly line—to be priest. Both actions went against God's law (Judges 17).

The group of returnees who did not have family records to prove their status were probably genuine. But due to a lack of proof, the leaders exercise caution (Ezra 2:62). Zerubbabel orders them not to eat "any of the most sacred food" (v. 63). This food was part of the temple offerings and was reserved for priests (Leviticus 2:3, 10).

It was an offence for a person with uncertain priestly credentials to do what only priests were allowed to do, as there was always the possibility that people would claim to be priests to benefit from the religious system in Israel. While priests did not inherit any land, they were provided for through the temple offerings and tithes. In the confusion of a large group of people returning home, some with baser motives could take advantage of the situation to secure for themselves financial support for life. Given the lack of proper records, the only recourse was to determine the truth through the Urim and Thummim—likely stones on a high priest's breastplate that were used to find out what God was saying (Exodus 28:29–30).

It is good to take a moment to reflect on the fact that in the New Testament, through Christ's sacrifice and God's adoption of us, we are also "a holy priesthood" and "a royal priesthood" (1 Peter 2:5–9). **Our credentials come not from our ancestry, but our relationship with Christ.** By being united with Him, we can gladly come to the Lord's table to partake of the sacred meal that God has prepared for us. This is the amazing grace and mercy of God.

Think about the cautious approach taken for those who said they were priests but had insufficient credentials. How does it compare with the New Testament teaching that all believers belong to a holy priesthood (1 Peter 2:4–5)?

While we are all described as a priesthood of believers, Peter refers to himself as an "apostle" and "fellow elder" (1 Peter 1:1, 5:1), which indicate special leadership and ministry positions. Is there a place for some people to be in spiritual leadership in a congregation of priests in Christ? See 1 Timothy 3:1–10; Titus 1:6–9.

Day 6

Read Ezra 2:64–70

With exceptional administrative skill, the entire body of returnees has been categorised into sub-groups and carefully counted. Since only the men are counted, the actual number of people would have numbered more than 50,000; scholars have suggested as many as 235,000.[1] The people are well-organised and are ready to settle down and begin the great work of rebuilding the temple. They had been forced by their Babylonian conquerors to leave their homeland and stripped of everything, but now they return with possessions. Observes Bible commentator Adam Clarke: "Thus we find that God, in the midst of judgment, remembered mercy, and gave them favour in the land of their captivity."[2]

Arriving at the former site of Solomon's temple in Jerusalem must have been an exhilarating moment. There, some of the family heads give freewill offerings for the building project (Ezra 2:68). **These leaders are setting a good example for others: their giving is voluntary and generous, and they give according to their ability (v. 69).** Paul's instructions on Christian giving echo this spirit of giving: it should be voluntary, generous, and joyful (2 Corinthians 9:6–7). The churches in Macedonia went even further, giving sacrificially and beyond their ability (8:3) to help poorer fellow Christians in Judea. God is pleased with such generous giving, and often multiplies what is given for His work.

Today, if we were to visit war-torn areas such as Jaffna in the north of Sri Lanka, we would see many streets with houses in ruins, left behind by inhabitants who had fled in desperate conditions. Many have not returned, and the ruins stand as sad reminders of what used to be vibrant communities. Much of Judea must have been in a similar state of ruin after the destruction by the Babylonians.

The returnees from Babylon, however, bring new life to the land. Those who are to serve in the temple occupy Jerusalem and its neighbourhoods, while the rest of the people go back to their own towns (Ezra 2:70). It is a new day in the land of God's people. Indeed, nothing happens by chance or accident in God's kingdom. It was God's hand that brought the Israelites as captives into exile, as a result of their persistent idolatry (Deuteronomy 28:36–68; Daniel 1:2). But it was also His hand that brought a remnant of His people back to their land, as He had promised (Jeremiah 29:10). Nothing that happens is beyond God's control, and we must be thankful that it is so.

[1] David Guzik, "Commentary on Ezra 2:64–67", 2006, https://enduringword.com/bible-commentary/ezra-2/.
[2] Adam Clarke, "Commentary on Ezra 2:69", *The Adam Clarke Commentary* (1832), https://www.studylight.org/commentaries/acc/ezra-2.html.

Why is it good for giving to be voluntary? Why is it important for leaders to set a good example in the way they give their time and money? How is your giving?

How was God involved in the Israelites' exile and return to Jerusalem? What does this say about God's sovereignty, mercy, and love?

Day 7

Read Ezra 3:1–6

Altars feature prominently in Scripture. The first thing that Noah did when he came out of the ark was to build an altar (Genesis 8:20). Abraham did the same when he reached Canaan (12:7).

The altar was a central object in the tabernacle and temple, as commanded by God (Exodus 27:1–8; 2 Chronicles 4:19). Sacrifices made on it allowed worshippers to find forgiveness for their sins and to be reconciled with God. This sacrificial system of the Old Testament is fulfilled by Jesus: His sacrifice on the cross is an effective once-for-all atonement for our sins (Hebrews 9:11–28; 10:1–14; 13:10–12).

As Christians, we are a priesthood of believers who are called to offer spiritual sacrifices (1 Peter 2:5), not on a physical altar but as a spiritual act of worship (Romans 12:1). Although we no longer have to burn sacrifices on a physical altar, the Old Testament altar remains an important reminder of our salvation in Christ and our daily discipleship in Him. Our spiritual sacrifices include our dedication of ourselves and all that we have to God, as evidenced by how we worship, love, and serve God.

In the book of Ezra, even before the Jews build the temple, they build the altar; such is its importance (Ezra 3:2). Once they have settled into their towns, they make their first pilgrimage to Jerusalem during the seventh month, the most important month in the Jewish calendar. It is the month when the Day of Atonement, the Feast of Trumpets, and the Feast of Tabernacles are observed.

The Jews gather "as one" (v. 1), meaning they are united in purpose to build the temple and worship God. The altar is built, with Joshua and the priests taking the lead, supported by governor Zerubbabel (v. 2). They locate the foundations of the former altar and build a new altar on its site (v. 3), thus honouring the place that God had chosen for the temple and altar (2 Samuel 24:18; 1 Kings 9:3). At the altar, the people offer burnt offerings in the morning and evening, as stipulated in the law (Ezra 3:3; Numbers 28:1–8). They also celebrate the Feast of the Tabernacles, an important festival during which they dwelt in temporary shelters that recalled their exodus journey (Numbers 29:12–39). Having returned from their exile, this was of special importance to them.

Not all is well, however. The Jews suffer from "their fear of the peoples around them" (Ezra 3:3). They sense hostility in their neighbours, which will threaten their building project. Nevertheless, it is a happy occasion, for they have restored the worship of God (vv. 4–6).

The Christian life involves "offering spiritual sacrifices acceptable to God through Jesus Christ" (1 Peter 2:5). There is an inner altar in our hearts where we offer ourselves, our time, heart, mind, and treasures to God. We must ensure that this altar is not forgotten or ignored.

Why was the altar important in Old Testament worship? What is its significance in the New Testament? See Romans 12:1; Hebrews 13:15–16; and 1 Peter 2:5. What does this say about the centrality of the cross of Jesus and the crucified life He calls us to live? See Luke 9:23 and Mark 8:35.

The people restored their worship before they embarked on rebuilding the temple. What spiritual principle can you learn from this? What would it mean for us today to restore our worship?

Day 8

Read Ezra 3:7–9

In his book, *Fire in the Fireplace*, author Charles Hummel suggests that the fire (renewal by the Holy Spirit) needs a fireplace (church). It is possible to have a fireplace without fire—a church that has not been renewed by the Holy Spirit and is therefore dead and useless. Conversely, fire (spiritual revival and its manifestations) without a fireplace (the church with its proper ordering and accountability) can burn out of control and cause damage.

So, now that the Jews have restored worship, they commence rebuilding the temple so that their worship can have a proper home as stipulated by God's law. They assemble and pay the masons and carpenters to start work on the temple (Ezra 3:7). They also pay, in kind, the people of Sidon and Tyre for good-quality cedar logs to be brought in by sea (v. 7). This is reminiscent of what King Solomon did when he built the first temple (2 Chronicles 2:3–10).

Work on the temple begins in the second month of the second year (Ezra 3:8). Note that the site of the temple was called "the house of God in Jerusalem" even before the temple was built; God was already present at the site which He had chosen long ago. Starting the building work in the second month is again reminiscent of Solomon's building of the first temple, which also began in the second month (1 Kings 6:1). These are clues that the Jews, while lacking the kind of resources that Solomon had, want very much to restore the temple to its original glory.

The building work needs close supervision, so the Levites who are well-versed in temple furnishings and worship—and who are 20 years and above—are appointed to be "site supervisors" (Ezra 3:8). Under the law of Moses, Levites began serving at the temple at the age of 30 (Numbers 4:3, 23, 30), but King David revised it to 20 (1 Chronicles 23:24). Such careful supervision shows the Israelites' desire to build a temple of quality according to God's instructions. That the Levites "joined together" (Ezra 3:9) in their task speaks of close coordination and a sense of unity. How good and pleasant it must have been (Psalm 133:1)!

Today, there is no temple in Jerusalem. Instead, in Christ we are all corporately and individually the temple of God. We are "God's building" (1 Corinthians 3:9, 16; 6:19). As a congregation, we are being built up by God to rise up "to become a holy temple in the Lord" (Ephesians 2:21–22). We must recognise this as we submit ourselves to the "rebuilding activity" of God in our lives as individuals and as a church. This is a glorious project of God, and every one of us is involved in it.

The Bible says that we are God's house (Hebrews 3:6). What lessons can we learn from this passage in Ezra on why it is necessary for us to ensure that in our personal and congregational lives, there is a rebuilding process going on?

Consider your own experience in "joining together" (Ezra 3:9) with others to serve God. What are some challenges you have encountered and what are the joys you have experienced?

Day 9

Read Ezra 3:10–13

Having laid the foundations for the new temple in Jerusalem, the Jews have reason to celebrate and praise God loudly. God has kept His promise by bringing them back to the holy city. Now, they are standing on the threshold of rebuilding the temple, which will give them a spiritual and national identity.

The temple had always been the very centre of Israel's national and religious life. It was located in the one place of worship God had chosen (Deuteronomy 12:4–7). It was there that God put His Name (v. 5). And it was around that Name, associated with the temple, that Israel would find its national and spiritual unity and focus. Now, against all odds, what many may have thought would never happen is unfolding right before their eyes. The priests put on their ceremonial garments as trumpets and cymbals are brought out to make joyful music to the Lord. It is time to praise and thank the Lord. They had not been able to do this for 70 years.

They sing, "He is good; his love endures for ever", from the hymnbook of Israel (Psalm 107:1; 118:1). This is the same song that was sung at the dedication of the first temple (2 Chronicles 7:3). This time, the gathering is humbler, but their joy is no less. There are exuberant shouts of joy.

There are some, however, who weep, for they feel pain even amid the joy. These are the older men: priests, Levites, and family heads who had seen the original temple in its glory (Ezra 3:12). They may have also stood there years ago, watching their beloved temple go up in flames and be utterly destroyed by the Babylonian army. **For them, this occasion recalls lots of painful memories, and perhaps the realisation that despite doing their best to build a new temple, they would not be able to match the glory and beauty of the former one.** Unable to control their emotions, they weep loudly, though the others cannot distinguish between the joyful shouts and their painful cries (v. 13).

While the weeping of the seniors is understandable, such reactions come with potential danger. As Bible teacher G. Campbell Morgan reminds us in his book, *Searchlights from the Word*, "The backward look which discounts present activity is always a peril."[3] Nostalgia can hinder faithful enterprise.

Worshipping God should bring joy to our hearts and unite us. Renewing worship to keep it fresh is something we should all be concerned about.

Sometimes, there are differences in opinion between older and younger people in this regard. It is important to listen to the wisdom and experience of older Christians—while keeping in mind that nostalgia about how things used to be should not become an obstacle to new pathways of renewal. It is God who leads and unites us.

[3] G. Campbell Morgan, *Searchlights from the Word*, (Eugene, Oregon: Wipf & Stock, 2010), 144.

Think about your reactions to starting a great project in your life or in your church. What gave you hope and joy? How can you maintain such a response throughout the process?

In what ways can seniors bring wisdom to the work of God? When must they be careful that their perspective does not dampen the efforts of others? What are the implications for you, whatever your age?

Day 10

Read Ezra 4:1–5

When we faithfully carry out God's work, Satan will often stand against us. This is to be expected, as he opposes anything that would bring glory to God. The Bible identifies Satan as "your enemy" (1 Peter 5:8) or "adversary" (ESV).

In today's reading, the same word is used for the "enemies of Judah and Benjamin" (Ezra 4:1). These people are local residents in Samaria (to the north of Judea) who were brought in by the Assyrian king Esarhaddon after he conquered the northern kingdom of Israel in 722 BC (v. 2; 2 Kings 17:22–24). Many had intermarried with the remaining Jews. Though an Israelite priest had been sent to educate them in the ways of God, they continued to worship their own gods, practising a syncretistic (mixed) religion which dishonoured the Lord and produced new forms of idolatry (2 Kings 17:27–41). These are the enemies who are now trying to disrupt God's work.

They offer to help the building project and claim to worship God (Ezra 4:2). But the leaders of the Jews see through their ploy and tell them, "You have no part with us in building a temple to our God" (v. 3). They have enough discernment to spot spiritual danger. Had they gone ahead and accepted the help of their unspiritual enemies, the work would have suffered and God would have been dishonoured. Idolatry would have crept in, and the enemies would have claimed that the temple was the work of their hands.

In the New Testament, Simon the Sorcerer in Samaria (the same place that many of these enemies came from) offered the apostles Peter and John money to give him the spiritual power they possessed. Peter rebuked him, saying, "You have no part or share in this ministry, because your heart is not right before God" (Acts 8:21). That is the problem with those who slyly offer to help the Jews with their building project: their hearts are not right with God, and they are not really worshippers of God.

The leaders give a reasonable answer to their enemies. Cyrus had authorised only the Jewish returnees to build the temple (Ezra 4:3). Spurned, the enemies begin psychological warfare, finding ways to threaten and discourage the Jews by bribing officials to impede the work (vv. 4–5).

We should not be surprised to encounter opposition of various kinds when we are faithfully carrying out God's work. They can come either as hostile actions or friendly offers that hide subtle spiritual dangers. Satan can be like a "roaring lion" (1 Peter 5:8) as well as a deceiving "angel of light" (2 Corinthians 11:14). In the first case, we need faithfulness and courage. In the second, we need vigilance and discernment, with the help of the Holy Spirit and the counsel of the godly.

How might Satan use human beings as his agents? Why do you think Jesus taught His disciples to pray, "deliver us from the evil one" (Matthew 6:13)?

What are the dangers of joining hands with those whose hearts are not right with God in doing God's work (2 Corinthians 6:14)?

Day 11

Read Ezra 4:6–16

The narrative breaks off here and moves forward a few decades. We know that this passage refers to later events because the Persian kings mentioned, Xerxes (the same as Ahaseurus in Esther) and Artaxerxes (the king at the time of Nehemiah), came to power long after the reign of Cyrus.

By this time, the Jews have rebuilt the temple and have started repairing the walls and the rest of the city. However, their enemies persist in trying to obstruct their progress. Today's reading shows us how chronic the opposition to God's work was. **The resistance that the Jews face is not a one-off event, but a perennial spiritual situation.**

The enemies of the Jews complain to the Persian kings, dispatching a formal letter to Artaxerxes accusing the Jews of acting treacherously against the king (Ezra 4:6). The letter is crafted with political and psychological shrewdness. The host of leaders who sign the letter stress their impressive credentials and claim to have the popular support of the king's subjects in the province of Trans-Euphrates, of which Judea was a part (vv. 9–10). They inform the king that the troublesome Jews are now "restoring the walls and repairing the foundations" of Jerusalem (v. 12). They then call Jerusalem "that rebellious and wicked city" (v. 12), and suggest that historical records will prove how troublesome and rebellious the city had been in the past (v. 15). If the city is rebuilt, they claim, the consequences for the king and his empire would be grave. The city would stop paying taxes and royal revenue would be adversely affected (v. 13). The king, they warn, "will be left with nothing in Trans-Euphrates" (v. 16).

The writers claim to be loyal citizens who have the king's interests uppermost in their minds, and are therefore under obligation to report to the king what is going on. It is all intended to make the king react angrily against the Jews. God's servants may be falsely accused from time to time. Jesus himself was falsely accused (Matthew 26:59–60); so was Moses (Numbers 16:13), Paul (Acts 21:28), and so many others.

Perhaps this passage is speaking to a situation you may be facing today—at home, at your workplace, or in church. You may be accused of something you did not do, or your motives are being questioned and maligned. This can be very discouraging, and it may seem easier to pursue the path of least resistance—but this may lead you away from what God has asked you to do. If you are experiencing false accusations, take courage and comfort, because God has promised to protect you against hostile weapons and words, for this is "the heritage of the servants of the LORD" (Isaiah 54:17).

Was there any truth to the enemies' accusations of the Jews? Have you experienced facts being twisted by Satan to work against God's forgiven children? What was your reaction?

How can the enemy bring fear into the hearts of God's children? How can you counteract this if it happens to you?

Day 12

Read Ezra 4:17–24

Setbacks are difficult to accept, especially when we are faithfully doing God's work. Why does a ministry initiative fizzle out? Why does a ministry team member die tragically? Why do we have to close down an important ministry? In such situations, it may seem that Satan is having a laugh at the expense of God's people. And this seems to be the case in today's reading.

Just as the enemies of the Jews had hoped, the king replies to their letter of accusation against the Jews by issuing a "stop-work" order. A search of historical records has been made, and Jerusalem has indeed been found to have "a long history of revolt against kings and has been a place of rebellion and sedition" (Ezra 4:19). As far as colonising empires are concerned, Jerusalem is a troublemaker. Moreover, under its former kings David and Solomon, Jerusalem had once been the capital of a large and powerful united kingdom in the region, commanding tribute from lesser nations around them (v. 20). The potential for Jerusalem to rise from the ashes and reclaim such a powerful position is seen as a "threat" (v. 22) to the Persian king.

To prevent this threat from growing, the king orders all building work in the city to halt (v. 21). This would have delighted the enemies of the Jews. Their plan has come to fruition, and they have effectively tied the hands of the Jews, who now face grave danger if they continue rebuilding the city. The eagerness of the enemies can be seen in how hastily they set out to implement the king's order—note the words, "As soon as" and "immediately" (v. 23)—and "compelled them by force to stop" (v. 23). Imagine the scene: perhaps they pull down the work platforms, seize the building tools, and station soldiers to arrest or kill anyone who would dare to disobey the king. It is clear that some degree of force is used against the Jews, who must have protested.

The narrative that breaks off in verse 5 then continues in verse 24. Just as the building of the city is stopped by royal decree, the building of the temple "came to a standstill until the second year of the reign of Darius king of Persia" (v. 24). **For a period of some 15 years, no building sounds are heard at the temple site, much to the satisfaction of the enemies of God's people. What will God do next, we wonder?**

It may seem that Satan is laughing at God's children, having successfully stopped them from doing God's

work. Have you been in a situation like this? You can be sure that Satan has a hand in it, but you can also be sure that God has the upper hand in all such situations. The Bible encourages us to be "joyful in hope, patient in affliction, faithful in prayer" (Romans 12:12). God knows and sees all that we are facing.

How should God's people relate to governing authorities? How should Christians respond if a law of the land forbids Christian mission?

What evidence is there that God's work within us is well under way? Or has the work stopped because of our disobedience, lack of faith, or fear? What would you do about those places where the work seems to have come to a standstill?

Day 13

Read Ezra 5:1–2

English preacher Charles Spurgeon wrote about the comfort that God's children have from knowing that God is sovereign: "Under the most adverse circumstances, in the most severe trials, they believe that sovereignty has ordained their afflictions, that sovereignty overrules them, and that sovereignty will sanctify them all."

The Jews receive a "stop-work" order from earthly authorities and enemies, but the heavenly king sends them a "resume work" order. The order from heaven's throne supersedes that from the throne on earth. God's order came through two prophets, Haggai and Zechariah (Ezra 5:1), whose messages are recorded in the Bible.

Haggai finds the Jews in a spiritually lethargic state. They give various excuses for not carrying out God's orders, saying, for example, that it is not the right time to build the temple (Haggai 1:2). But the prophet asks: How they can build such nice houses for themselves when the house of the Lord remains in ruins (v. 4)? He exhorts them to "give careful thought" to their ways—a phrase he uses five times (1:5, 7; 2:15, 18). Haggai's message is: think carefully and work faithfully. The Lord assures the leaders and people that He is with them (1:13; 2:4), and stirs up their spirits as He had done in Babylon (1:14; Ezra 1:5). Bolstered by such prophetic words and divine action, the people return to the work (Haggai 1:14–15) and finish building the temple.

Through Zechariah (his name means "YHWH remembered"), God sends a message expressing his anger against the nations. He says: "I will return to Jerusalem with mercy, and there my house will be rebuilt" (Zechariah 1:14–16). With a series of inspiring visions of the future temple, the prophet delivers the message that God will enable His people to complete the temple building. Just as Zerubbabel's hands had laid the foundations, his hands will also complete the building (4:8–9), because it will be accomplished not by human might or power but by God's Spirit (4:6).

Encouraged by these messages from the two prophets, the leaders and the people resume the building work (Ezra 5:2).

God sends Haggai and Zechariah during the time when a new king, Darius, ascends the Persian throne amid political troubles. Darius is too busy to look into the Jerusalem matter and the Jews complete the temple building. God shows His strong hand and intervenes accordingly, just as He does today when we face discouragement and disappointment.

Devotional writer Oswald Chambers once wrote, "We have to pray with our eyes on God, not on our difficulties." God can overrule our obstacles and frustrations and work His sovereign interventions in our lives. We have to remember that God rules over all and will ensure that His work is accomplished as we trust Him prayerfully and work faithfully. When we are discouraged, He often sends His servants to encourage us.

Recall occasions in the past when God sent a special word to encourage you to continue doing something that you had stopped out of discouragement or fear. How did you respond?

God can intervene strongly, changing rulers, sending prophets, and challenging people. Is He sending you to help with someone's spiritual walk today?

Day 14

Read Ezra 5:3–10

As soon as the work in the temple resumes, there is an official inquiry. The local Persian governor and his officials visit the construction site, wanting to know who authorised the rebuilding and the names of those involved in the work (Ezra 5:3–4). Perhaps the Jews' enemies instigated the officials' actions.

Fifteen years after the work had ceased, the officials may have changed, but they still fear getting into trouble should the new Persian king, their overlord, come to hear about the temple. In their actions, though, this batch of officials are less antagonistic than the corrupt officials the Samaritans had paid to put a stop to the work during the reign of King Cyrus (Ezra 4:5). They seem to be simply doing their job. Of course, even in such circumstances, they are a potential obstacle to the work of God.

God is with His people: "But the eye of their God was watching over the elders of the Jews, and they were not stopped until a report could go to Darius and his written reply be received" (5:5).

The letter sent by the officials reports their investigation of the building of the new temple in Jerusalem. It tells of how they questioned the Jews and secured the names of those involved, in case the king wants to check their background to see if they are troublemakers. The description of the temple construction gives us hints about the dedication and efficiency of the temple builders: "The work is being carried on with diligence and is making rapid progress" (v. 8). That, combined with the phrase "the temple of the great God", is meant to indicate the urgency and importance of the situation. However, above all the bureaucracy of empire is in the hand of a God whose eyes and ears are attentive to His people (Psalm 34:15), as we shall see in tomorrow's reading.

Sometimes, we may feel that we are like a little cog in a giant complex machine. **Who would notice the ordinary people or the marginalised? We may feel forgotten, but God does not ignore us.** He knows every person, both great and small, in the world. No one is hidden from His eyes. This should be a comforting truth for His children, for the "eyes of the LORD are on the righteous, and his ears are attentive to their cry" (Psalm 34:15; 1 Peter 3:12). And "he who watches over Israel will neither slumber nor sleep" (Psalm 121:4).

The Bible says that God's eye was watching over His people (Ezra 5:5). What does that mean? Read Exodus 3:7–10 to examine what God told Moses. How does this comfort you today?

How can our work for the Lord retain its enthusiasm and faithfulness even if we have to face official bureaucracy and other forms of difficulty?

Day 15

Read Ezra 5:11–17

Is our mission as Christians being suppressed by the fear of opposition? Today, we look at the Jews' reply to the official inquiry as described in the letter the regional officials send to King Darius. From the Jews' reply, we learn a few things about how to respond to opposition we may face when we are doing God's work.

First, the Jews state their identity and vocation. "We are the servants of the God of heaven and earth, and we are rebuilding the temple" (Ezra 5:11). **Their statement reminds us of how important it is to hold fast to our identity and mission in a distracting and dangerous world.** Carelessness, busyness, and lack of courage can erode one's identity and vocation.

Second, the Jews provide more history to support their case (v. 11). It is always good to ensure that the church retains its memory. The Jews explain why their temple had been destroyed—they had angered God, who handed them over to the Babylonian conquerors (v. 12). They acknowledge the blame, confessing the sins of their fathers. They know they had acted unfaithfully and God had taken proper action.

Third, the Jews relate how King Cyrus had issued an edict for them to return to Jerusalem from Babylon and rebuild the temple. He had also returned the temple objects that had been seized by the Babylonians and appointed Sheshbazzar (probably Zerubbabel) as governor of Judea and leader of the rebuilding project—which, though it had begun, remains uncompleted.

The provincial officials, who realise the Jews may have a case, request that the king make a decision on whether the temple construction should be allowed to continue. They suggest that the royal archives be searched to see if King Cyrus had indeed issued the edict that the Jews referred to (v. 17). The implication is that if there is such a royal decree, then it still carries weight and needs to be honoured. There are examples of churches and mission agencies whose existence and work have been saved by archival material. I remember how a church archivist had to travel to America to search for a piece of paper that eventually exempted the church from paying a development charge of millions of dollars. How we need church historians and archivists!

We may experience unreasonable opposition when doing God's work. But we should not be discouraged; instead, we are to prayerfully try to overcome our difficulties. It helps to remember our identity, vocation, and history as the people of God. We can then calmly and respectfully explain our position so that those who seem to be opposing us may understand—and perhaps change their minds.

Why is it important to remember our identity, vocation, and history? How are these connected with one another? How would you summarise your identity and vocation?

What would you say to someone who asks you why you have hope in Christ (1 Peter 3:15)?

Day 16

Read Ezra 6:1–12

Have you ever had trouble finding something that is missing? It may feel like you are looking for a needle in a haystack. It might have felt like that when Darius orders a search to be made for records related to Cyrus' earlier decree. But imagine the staff in the royal archives searching the records, and the Holy Spirit working invisibly among them, leading them to the right document!

A scroll is found in the city of Ecbatana (probably a summer royal residence) and is presented to King Darius, who issues a decree accordingly. The contents of his letter to the local officials are unbelievably advantageous to the Jews. Hence their joy that God has changed the attitude of the king (Ezra 6:22).

Darius' letter mentions the contents of the scroll that records Cyrus' decree allowing the temple in Jerusalem to be built as a place of worship and sacrifice (vv. 2–3). The gold and silver temple articles returned to the Jews were to be placed in the temple (v. 5), and the costs of the rebuilding were to be paid from the royal treasury. Darius' decree also states the dimensions of the temple—about 27 metres high and 27 metres wide, "with three courses of large stones and one of timber" (vv. 3–4). This represented

the maximum size allowed and the strong foundations that could withstand earthquakes.[4]

Furthermore, Darius orders the temple construction to proceed without any interference (v. 7). The expenses are to be fully paid from provincial taxes (v. 8), and all that is needed for the sacrifices in the temple are to be provided daily (v. 9) so that the sacrifices and prayers for the king and his sons (reflecting personal interests) might continue. Anyone who interrupts the work is to be severely punished (vv. 11–12). God has surely intervened so that the work will not be interrupted. **What initially seemed to be a setback is turning out to be something that speeds up and facilitates the work instead.** In the words of English poet William Cowper, "The clouds which ye so much dread, Are big with mercy."[5]

When the early church in Jerusalem suffered persecution and its leaders Peter and John were forbidden to preach the name of Jesus, it looked like it was "game over". But God intervened and the Jewish religious leaders let Peter and John go because they could not decide how to punish them, and because people were praising God for their ministry. Subsequently, the apostles were beaten and Stephen was martyred. As a result of the persecution, the believers were scattered, but God had an unchangeable plan: the scattering became the very means of the rapid spread of the gospel beyond Jerusalem.

The battle may seemingly be lost at times, but with God, the spiritual war will always be won, whether in our personal lives or in the life of the church.

[4] Matthew Poole, "Commentary on Ezra 6:3", *Matthew Poole's Commentary*, 1st ed., accessed 1 June 2018, http://biblehub.com/commentaries/poole/ezra/6.htm.
[5] Quoted in Derek Kidner, *Ezra and Nehemiah* (Leiscester, Downers Grove: Inter-Varsity Press, 1979), 57.

Picture the search being made of the royal archives for records of Cyrus' decree, and how God was working as the letters between Darius and the officials went back and forth. God's hand cannot be restricted by geography or bureaucracy. How does knowing this influence the way we trust God and pray to Him?

Read Romans 8:28. How much do you believe that God is at work in all things, putting everything together for the good of those who are called by Him and who love Him?

Day 17

Read Ezra 6:13–18

God cannot be stopped. It is His will that the Jews rebuild the temple, so with the king's support, the building project proceeds without further interruption. Upon receipt of the royal decree, the provincial authorities "carried it out with diligence" (Ezra 6:13). And the people, inspired by the preaching of the prophets Haggai and Zechariah, complete the building (v. 14).

Royal decrees and official assistance are not enough; the people have to be motivated from within to complete the work. **Favourable circumstances must be matched with faithful character and fervent commitment.** All this is provided by God, who facilitates in every way the successful completion of His house.

The temple is completed in 516 BC, four years after the work resumes (and after 15 years of inactivity). It is a long and difficult process, but when the building is finally completed, there is a great celebration. The temple is dedicated joyfully (v. 16), with sacrifices and offerings made in keeping with the joyful and holy moment. Sin offerings are made for each of the 12 tribes (v. 17); the remnant representing the entire nation of Israel. The priests and Levites are installed in their various groups, ready to serve the Lord in His temple (v. 18).

Long ago, the Jewish captives were covered with shame and heartbreak as they saw Jerusalem and the temple destroyed. Eventually, however, they returned with hope, and now, they celebrate joyfully a new temple on the same site, ready to be used for the worship of God. God has kept His promise, showing that He is with His people and has removed their shame.

The dedication service is reminiscent of the dedication of the first temple built by King Solomon (2 Chronicles 5:2–7:10). This time, the ceremony is simpler and carried out in humbler circumstances, but the joy is no less. Christian historian Edwin Yamauchi notes that there are some things missing.[6] Prominent among them is the ark, which had been lost in the Babylonian captivity. Also, there is only one menorah instead of the ten in Solomon's temple (see 2 Chronicles 4:7). Surviving Roman artwork depicts this menorah being carried away after the destruction of the temple in AD 70.

Perhaps it is a reminder that while God will forgive and restore if people confess their sins and repent, some things may be lost permanently as a consequence of sin. It is better to

obey God. Nevertheless, God promises to restore the glory of His temple in greater measure (Haggai 2:9). His presence is what gives the temple its glory, not the furnishings.

God can produce favourable circumstances to help us do His work of restoration and renewal. But this has to be matched by godly character and firm commitment to God on our part. If we do our work with humility and faith, God will honour our faith and obedience with His glory in our lives.

[6] Edwin Yamauchi and Elaine Phillips, *Ezra, Nehemiah, Esther* (Grand Rapids: Zondervan, 2017), Ezra 6:15.

Why is it important that favourable circumstances be matched by faithful character and fervent commitment? What happens if any of these are missing?

Why is it better to avoid sinning and disobeying God? What can be lost even though we experience forgiveness of our sins? Yet how can we lean on God to restore our lives?

Day 18

Read Ezra 6:19–22

After dedicating the temple, the worshippers dedicate themselves to God. Three insights can be gleaned from this.

First, there is obedience in the way they observe their first Passover celebration in the rebuilt temple. According to the law of Moses, it is to be observed on the 14th day of the first month (Ezra 6:19; Numbers 28:16). The returnees are careful to obey the law and its stipulations: the priests and Levites ensure that they are ceremonially clean by purifying themselves, thus respecting God and His law (Ezra 6:20). As with the first Passover during the Exodus, Passover lambs are slain and eaten communally (vv. 20–21; Exodus 12:21–28). A week-long Feast of the Unleavened Bread is also celebrated (Ezra 6:22). The Jews who celebrate Passover in the new temple would remember how their forebears were saved by God long ago, and be thankful that He had also saved them from the exile.

What significance does the Passover observance in the Old Testament have for Christians today? We know from the New Testament that the Passover ceremonies point to Christ, "our Passover Lamb" (1 Corinthians 5:7) who was sacrificed for our salvation. Christians commemorate this truth by sharing the Lord's Supper instituted by Christ. When He provided a Passover meal for His disciples, He said, "Take and eat; this is my body" (Matthew 26:26), and "do this in remembrance of me" (1 Corinthians 11:24).

Second, the worshippers focus on holiness. Not only do the priests and Levites wash themselves to become ceremonially clean, but the people also separate themselves from the "unclean practices" of their Gentile neighbours (Ezra 6:21). Anyone who wishes to share the Passover meal is to do the same. **This means that the door is open to outsiders provided they seek God and become part of the covenant community, committing themselves to godly living;** compare this with how some foreigners are allowed to celebrate the Passover in Exodus 12:48–49. The Lord's Supper in church follows the same principles.

Third, it is a joyful celebration (Ezra 6:22). The worshippers are joyful that God has changed the king's heart. There is solemnity in keeping an important religious festival, but also deep joy. The early Christians similarly broke bread with joy and sincerity (Acts 2:46). We should do likewise; the joy should come as we remember God and His loving character and actions.

The worshippers of God are expected to show obedience, holiness, and joy in their lives.

Why is it important to gather in our places of worship to worship God? What attitudes should there be in our hearts as we do so?

What signs can you find of obedience, holiness, and joy in your life? Which of these do you need more of?

Day 19

Read Ezra 7:1–10

The first six chapters of Ezra record the rebuilding of the temple under Zerubbabel's leadership over a period of some 22 years. The record ends on a joyful note and some 57 years pass, during which time the events recorded in the book of Esther take place. Then God sends Ezra the scribe and priest.

Care is taken to trace Ezra's genealogy back to Aaron, the chief priest during the time of Moses (Ezra 7:1–5). Why does God send Ezra to Jerusalem? While Zerubbabel and Nehemiah are governors, Ezra is a learned teacher of the law (v. 6). When God led His people to build the new temple, the focus of His actions was on the proper worship of Him. **Now, in sending Ezra, God is bringing another focus—His Word. His people need to be taught His Word so that they can know Him and live faithfully.**

Ezra is eminently equipped by God for the task. Verse 10 is a significant description of this man, for it shows him devoting himself to doing three things. First, the study of God's law. Here is a man who soaks himself in God's Word, examining its details and understanding its message. It is not only an intellectual exercise but also a deeply spiritual quest to know God intimately. This is shown in Ezra's second task, which is observing the law. He seeks to be obedient; he is a practising student of God's Word (see James 1:22; Matthew 7:24). Third, he is committed to teaching God's Word, an activity he is greatly skilled at. Ezra is a careful scholar, a committed disciple, and a gifted teacher. He is said to "have stamped Israel with its lasting character as the people of a book."[7]

Ezra and his company are the second significant group to return to Judea. After the first group of Jews return in 538 BC, King Artaxerxes, the successor to Xerxes (Ahasuerus) who had married Esther (Esther 2), gives Ezra permission to lead this second group back to Judea (Ezra 7:6–7). The journey, which is about 1,600 km long, takes four months (v. 9; 7:11–8:36 gives further details about this journey). A recurring phrase is "the gracious hand of his God was on him" (7:9; see also 7:6, 28; 8:18, 22, 31). Ezra, God's man of the hour, arrives in Jerusalem in 458 BC, full of God's favour and strength.

God prepares His many servants for the tasks He has for them, according to His eternal purposes and plans. It is good to remember that not only does God call us for specific tasks and roles, but He also equips us for these. Perhaps you can reflect on how God has been guiding, preparing, and using you. You will find that there is a common thread that runs through these things—God's sovereign choice and grace. You may also recognise this in the lives of those around you.

7 Kidner, *Ezra and Nehemiah*, 62.

What is the relationship between worship and the Word? Which of these need strengthening in your life?

What can we learn from Ezra about how God prepares His instruments? Christ referred to Paul as "my chosen instrument" (Acts 9:15). How do you think God had trained Paul? Consider your own spiritual training.

Day 20

Read Ezra 7:11–28

Does God ever make use of earthly kings who are not believers to facilitate His work? Today's passage shows that He does.

When Ezra returns, he has in his possession a letter of authorisation from the king (Ezra 7:11). Personally addressed to Ezra, it decrees that any Jewish priest or Levite who wishes to accompany Ezra is permitted to do so (v. 13). Ezra is to assess the situation in Judea and Jerusalem with regard to the law of Moses (v. 14), and to ensure that the law is understood and obeyed, and that proper worship of God in the temple and a judicial system according to the law is established.

Ezra is not being sent empty-handed; he is supplied with gold and silver from the royal treasury (v. 15). He is also authorised to collect contributions from the province of Babylon and freewill offerings from the people (v. 16). This is to be used to pay for various sacrifices in the Jerusalem temple (v. 17). The remainder of the money is to be used at the discretion of Ezra and the leaders as God directs them (v. 18). Further, Ezra is authorised to collect contributions from the provincial leaders (vv. 21–24; this part of the letter is addressed to treasurers of the Trans-Euphrates). But he is not allowed to collect taxes from the priests, Levites, and temple workers (v. 24).

Ezra is amply provided for, so that the worship in the temple is not hindered in any way. The king takes care to ensure that God's commands are carried out by the Jews "with diligence" (v. 23). The motive for the great lengths to which Artaxerxes goes is stated: "Why should [God's] wrath fall on the realm of the king and of his sons?" (v. 23). This was also the motive of Cyrus and the other Persian kings; they had sought to placate the local gods in their realm for their own wellbeing, but God uses this self-interest for His own eternal purposes. Ezra recognises this and attributes the king's goodwill to the work of God in Artaxerxes' heart (vv. 27–28). Surely "in the LORD's hand the king's heart is a stream of water that he channels towards all who please him" (Proverbs 21:1).

Ezra is also authorised to set up a legal system to administer justice according to the law of Moses and to punish those who break the law (vv. 25–26). He is also to teach the law to the people (v. 25). Ezra recognises that the hand of his God is on him and is greatly encouraged (v. 28).

Many things in our lives, like travel visas, loans, scholarships, and job applications, may be decided by authorities who may not be believers in our Lord. **It is good to remember that God rules over all and can also overrule. God can use such authorities to fulfil His purposes in our lives, and we must not forget to pray.** We may be surprised at how He can answer our prayers beyond our imagination.

When things work out well and you feel the favour of everyone, who do you think is at work? How would this motivate you to obey God fully?

The king's letter focused on right worship and proper justice according to God's law. How would you assess your worship and obedience of God, and help others to do the same?

Day 21

Read Ezra 8:1–14

Encouraged by all that God has done to create favourable circumstances and positive attitudes from the powers that be, Ezra gathers leaders from the Jewish community in Babylon to accompany him to Jerusalem. Both Ezra and Nehemiah are excellent administrators and disciplined leaders. They keep proper records to ensure proper governance. In this passage, Ezra lists the names of the Jewish leaders in his group (Ezra 8:1–14).

It is a sizeable group—not as large as the first group that accompanied Zerubbabel (a descendant of David who continues the royal line and is named in the genealogy of Jesus in Matthew 1:13 and Luke 3:27) but nevertheless a large enough number. According to Ezra's records, there are 1,496 men. If women and children are included (Ezra 8:21), the total number of returnees would have been about 6,000 to 7,000 people, according to some Bible scholars[8].

Though the names may not mean much to the modern reader, the Jews in Ezra's time would have understood their significance. Many of the men came from prominent Jewish families, and the first few names include two priests and their relatives and a descendant of David. Bible commentator Derek Kidner notes that "in every case but one these groups are joining, at long last, the descendants of the pioneers from their own family stock, who had been in the first party to return from Babylon eighty years before. The family names in verses 4–14 can all (except Joab, verse 9) be found in 2:3–15."[9]

Kidner further observes that when the first group of returnees decided to accompany Zerubbabel to Jerusalem, some families may have been divided when some members went and some stayed. **Ezra brought with him family members who had originally chosen to remain in Babylon, and there must have been a joyful reunion of families in Jerusalem.** It shows us that God can give us second chances when we fail to act rightly, and that He loves to bring families together.

Through Ezra 7:28 to 9:15 (except for Ezra 8:35–36), Ezra writes with a personal "I" or "we". In his heart, he must have rejoiced that God had chosen to send others with him. God often ensures that we have company to encourage us when we do His work. Remember how Jesus chose 12 disciples to be with Him, and how He sent them and other disciples out two by two (Luke 6:13, 10:1).

Why do you think it is good to have partners in what we do for God? Reflect on your experience of working in teams and how it helped you and the others.

We saw how God loves to bring families together. Is there any practical application that you can think of for yourself or your church?

The church in Antioch sent Paul and Barnabas as a missionary team (Acts 13:2–3), and henceforth, Paul also had teams in his various missionary journeys.

God seldom sends us alone on a mission. He often sends others to work with us, to lessen our burden and to encourage us. Even if you feel alone, you are never alone, for there are others who are praying for you or supporting you in other ways. Take courage and give thanks to God for those who stand with you in life's tasks and challenges.

[8] David Guzik, *Enduring Word.*
[9] Kidner, *Ezra and Nehemiah*, 65.

Day 22

Read Ezra 8:15–30

Today's passage brings out two important lessons for us to consider. Firstly, we can fail to do God's bidding because of the fear of losing our present comfort or suffering inconveniences. The journey from Babylon to Jerusalem is about 1,600 km and takes four months. Along the way, the returnees camp near a place where they have to cross a canal (Ezra 8:15). There, an important discovery is made: there are no Levites among them (v. 15)! Not a single Levite has volunteered to return to Jerusalem. In the first group that returned with Zerubbabel, there had been very few Levites—only 74 out of about 50,000 men (2:40). This time, there are none.

Why is this the case? Perhaps the Levites are quite comfortable in Babylon. To return to Jerusalem and not inherit any land (Deuteronomy 18:1–2), and to exercise discipline and commitment in serving at the temple, would have seemed a daunting prospect. There is much to learn here as we remember missionary Jim Elliot's famous saying, "He is no fool who gives up what he cannot keep to gain what he cannot lose."

Troubled that there are no Levites in the group, Ezra decides to take action. How could the temple services proceed without an adequate number of Levites? **Though Artaxerxes had specifically permitted priests and Levites to return, there are no Levitical volunteers.** Ezra chooses some wise men of learning and sends them to Iddo, a leader in Kasiphia, a place where there are temple servants (Ezra 8:17). Ezra must have waited with concern for them to return. He realises that the gracious hand of God is still with him, because they return with 38 Levites and 220 temple servants, with a good leader, Sherebiah, among them (vv. 18–20).

The second key lesson is that we can trust God to protect us by praying to Him. Ezra, not taking things for granted, calls for a fast and prayer to ask God for a safe journey (v. 21). He feels that it would not be right to ask the king for a military escort, even though they are carrying large amounts of gold and silver. How could he, having told the king that God is with His people to protect them (v. 22)? God honours the prayers of the people (v. 23).

Ezra then distributes the gold, silver, and temple articles among the priests and Levites for safekeeping till they reach Jerusalem. To spread out the risk and share responsibility is a wise move. Ezra reminds them that they and the offerings are consecrated and belong to God

(v. 28). They are to guard the offerings carefully (v. 29). Even as we trust God to protect us, we are to take precautions and use wisdom to guard that which God has entrusted to us.

Ezra refused to request a military escort as he thought it would show a lack of faith in God. Nehemiah, however, accepted a military escort (Nehemiah 2:9). Did Nehemiah have less faith? In both cases, prayer was central. How should a Christian assess the right thing to do in such circumstances?

Reflect on the principles of sharing responsibility for the things that belong to God (e.g., church money and resources). What personal implications are there for you?

Day 23

Read Ezra 8:31–36

God does not fail His people, for they travel safely, even though dangers from enemies and bandits are present. Ezra repeats his favourite phrase here: the hand of God is on him and his people (Ezra 8:31; see 7:6, 28; 8:18, 22).

When they arrive in Jerusalem after a four-month journey, they rest three days (v. 32). The gold, silver, and sacred articles are then handed over to the priests and Levites in Jerusalem. "Everything was accounted for by number and weight, and the entire weight was recorded at that time" (v. 34). It may have been the practice of the Persian Empire to require such accounting and to send to the palace a certificate of receipt. In any case, the careful counting and weighing demonstrates the integrity and stewardship of Ezra and his associates, and the administrative effectiveness of the man.

Ezra's personal account continues in 9:1, but before that are two verses (8:35–36) that are written in the third person describing the offerings and sacrifices made by the new returnees at the temple. They offer two kinds of offerings: burnt offerings for the atonement for general sinfulness (Leviticus 1) and a sin offering for the forgiveness of specific sins (Leviticus 4). The burnt offerings include 12 bulls "for all Israel" (Ezra 8:35),

representing the 12 tribes of Israel. Likewise, the sin offering is 12 male goats. Though the two major tribes present are Judah and Benjamin, the others, such as Levi, also have their representatives in the remnant. God is dealing not just with part of the nation of Israel, but all of it. The people need to be reminded of their sinfulness and guilt as well as God's forgiveness and mercy. **This is always the basis of our relationship with God: a deep awareness of God's holiness and His mercy.**

Ezra hands over his credentials, letter, and decree of King Artaxerxes to the provincial rulers, who provide help to the temple and the people (v. 36). Ezra can now carry out his mission without any opposition or hindrance. His ministry of teaching will be featured more prominently in Nehemiah; the rest of his book will emphasise his efforts to establish God's law and reform the community.

Some of the lessons we can learn from today's passage include: We are to have integrity as part of good stewardship, exercising care and honesty over the things God has entrusted to us. The basis of our relationship with God is His holiness, mercy, and forgiveness in Christ.

How can we practise integrity in our personal lives, at home, in church, and at the workplace?

Paul wrote, "Consider therefore the kindness and sternness of God" (Romans 11:22). Why is it important to remember that the basis of our relationship with God is His holiness and mercy?

Day 24

Read Ezra 9:1–4

Ezra is in for a shock. He has come to teach the law and encourage the Jews to keep it, but finds out that the earlier returnees in Judea, who had arrived about 100 years ago, are living in disobedience to God. Instead of keeping themselves religiously and morally separate from their pagan neighbours, they have adopted some of their idolatrous practices (Ezra 9:1). This has happened primarily through intermarriage—a sin that the people, including the priests and Levites who should have known better, are guilty of (v. 2). A dangerous unfaithfulness and spiritual rot is establishing itself in the remnant community.

There is some similarity between the eight nations mentioned here (v. 1) and the seven nations mentioned in Deuteronomy 7:1, when the exodus community first arrived in the promised land. God has continually warned the Israelites not to mingle with these nations, so that they won't adopt their idolatrous practices. Unfortunately, intermarriage was frequently practised in Israel, even among the kings—for example, Solomon and Ahab. As a result, idolatry crept into the nation. This was one significant reason why God had handed the Israelites over to conquering armies, and why Jerusalem and its temple were destroyed.

Now that God has given His people a fresh start, it is deeply distressing to Ezra that they had not learnt from their past. The term "holy race" (Ezra 9:2) must not be misunderstood to mean that God's people (including Christians today) are to remain racially pure. **The focus here is not ethnic, but religious, purity.** David's great-grandmother was Ruth, a Moabitess who entered the covenant community by faith. The term "holy nation", used by the apostle Peter, included both believing Gentiles and Jews (1 Peter 2:9). The problem here is idolatry, which has serious consequences.

Ezra expresses his grief and anger by tearing his clothes and pulling out his hair and beard (Ezra 9:3). Stunned, he "sat down appalled". Those who share his sorrow sit down with him in fear, knowing that God's law has been disregarded. It is a sad day for Ezra.

It is easy for us to absorb the fallen world's ungodly patterns of thinking and behaviour into our way of life. Instead, we should look to the Holy Spirit for discernment, so that we can remain true to God by separating appropriately from the world's sinful ways (2 Corinthians 6:14–17), and by allowing the Spirit to transform our mind (Romans 12:2). Christ must be the only Lord of our lives, and we are to belong entirely to Him (14:8).

How can we end up compromising our spiritual and moral foundations in Christ when we associate with others not of the faith? As we live in pluralistic societies, how can we not be infected yet remain involved with others?

Reflect on Ezra's response to the news about the blatant sins of the people. What can we learn from him about how we should regard God's Word and commandments?

Day 25

Read Ezra 9:5–15

Ezra is genuinely distraught. Some may feel that the tearing of his clothes is mere superficial drama, but in today's passage, Ezra's prayer of lament, uttered on his knees and hands, reveals his sincere and deep distress (Ezra 9:5). Several truths can be seen here.

First, Ezra acknowledges his people's guilt. He confesses he is too ashamed to approach God as their sins are "higher than our heads" (v. 6); all of them are submerged in their sins.

Second, there is collective responsibility for the sins committed; note the use of the words "we" and "our" (v. 7).

Third, Israel suffers from chronic sinfulness, "From the days of our ancestors until now" (v. 7).

Fourth, it is because of this that Israel has suffered the tragic circumstances of national destruction and exile.

Fifth, God, however, in His mercy has given them a chance by bringing a "remnant" back to the land, moving the hearts of the Persian kings, and helping the people to build the new temple (vv. 8–9).

Sixth, yet the Jews seem to have blown this chance by repeating the sinful practice of intermarriage.

God had forbidden this because of the danger of spiritual apostasy and idolatry (Exodus 34:15–16). The land that the Israelites possess is polluted by idolatry and "detestable practices", which infect Israel through intermarriage (Ezra 9:11–12). Israel had already disregarded this divine commandment and paid the price for it in the past.

Seventh, the returning remnant is now facing the same danger, and there is no excuse whatsoever.

In the past, God had shown mercy by punishing the nation "less than our sins have deserved" (v. 13). If God had meted out appropriate punishment, the nation would have been wiped out. Instead, in His mercy, God preserved a remnant, a small portion of the original. The word "remnant" is mentioned three times in verses 13 to 15, emphasising how precarious the situation is. **God has saved a remnant to give them a chance, but now the remnant shows signs of the same sinfulness that had earlier brought punishment to the nation.** Will God punish again, and leave no remnant this time (v. 14)?

Admitting that no one can stand in the presence of God, Ezra indirectly cries out to God to be merciful even though His people have run out of excuses. Imagine a cancer eating away a vital organ of the body. After surgery, there is only enough of the organ left to survive. What if this remnant also shows signs of lingering cancer?

Read Isaiah 6:5. Why is the confession of sins both a personal and collective action? How can the sins of a few affect everyone?

Read Romans 7:21–25 and 1 John 3:6. What is the solution to chronic sinfulness? Why is it important for Christians not to keep on sinning? How can we avoid taking God's grace and mercy for granted (Romans 6:1–2)?

Day 26

Read Ezra 10:1–6

Have you ever been deeply moved by what someone said and how he said it? When the people see and hear Ezra praying his heartbroken prayer—the Hebrew text indicates that he repeatedly threw himself down in earnest prayer—it has a profound effect on the people. They gather around him and weep bitterly (Ezra 10:1), and Shekaniah, one of the leaders, steps forward to move the people from confession to restitution.

Shekaniah sees a way out; the depth of the people's confession gives him hope that the right steps can be taken in response to God's mercy and the work of the Spirit (v. 2). What he suggests is not an easy measure, especially to modern ears: he asks the people to make a covenant to put away their foreign wives and children.

Some have found this to be harsh. Why not, they wonder, ask the foreign wives to convert to the ways of the Lord? But would this have worked? Would this have preserved Israel's religious faithfulness? Most scholars accept that asking the foreign wives and children to leave was probably the most appropriate action. Bible scholar Adam Clarke suggests that the women and the children (it was better for the children to be with their mothers) were sent away with sufficient provisions: "Humanity must

have dictated this, and no law of God is contrary to humanity."[10] Also, it must be noted that there were probably not many children from such marriages (v. 44). It may also be that the Jewish men who had married foreign wives could have either divorced their Jewish wives or their actions may have created the problem of many unmarried Jewish women.

After Shekaniah expresses support for Ezra, the latter takes action (vv. 4–5). That Ezra is still deeply affected by the sinfulness of the people and their disregard of God's law can be seen in how he withdraws alone to one of the rooms in the temple and continues to fast and mourn (v. 6). He is close enough to God to feel God's grief so deeply.

Christians may not take sin seriously, but it affects their lives and the churches they attend (see 1 Corinthians 5:1–5). "To fear the LORD is to hate evil," notes Proverbs 8:13. God not only hates sin, but is also grieved by it. **We need to draw close to God so that we can feel the way He feels about sin and disobedience.** Along with that, we are to feel compassion for repentant sinners and find ways to help them be reconciled with God. Also, restitution and amends must be made where necessary. A repentant thief must return the stolen goods, while a converted liar should ask for forgiveness and clear the air with those who have heard his lies.

[10] Adam Clarke, "Commentary on 10:12", *The Adam Clarke Commentary* (1832), https://www.studylight.org/commentaries/acc/ezra-10.html.

Why do you think church prayer meetings are often poorly attended, even though we know revivals are always accompanied by heartfelt prayer and confession? How can we pray together in such a way that we are deeply moved by the Spirit?

Why is it important for restitution to be made for sins committed against God and others?

57

Day 27

Read Ezra 10:7–15

When a patient is diagnosed with a life-threatening illness, doctors will not delay in instituting drastic measures to save the patient. This is true in spiritual matters too.

The leaders in the community set into motion a process of repentance and renunciation. They start by summoning all to gather in Jerusalem, warning that failure to do so would result in the loss of membership in the community and property in the land (Ezra 10:7–8). The people meet, and are "greatly distressed by the occasion and because of the rain" (v. 9). There is "shivering misery"[11] that comes from both spiritual and physical discomfort.

Ezra then proceeds to speak clearly about their sin of intermarriage and the need to separate from (divorce) their foreign wives (v. 11). Responding together with a loud voice, the Israelites agree, but plead to be given time to settle the matter (v. 13). Standing in the rain seems to bother them as much as standing in guilt. Confessing that they "have sinned greatly" (v. 13), they suggest that time be taken to investigate those who have married foreign women.

Ezra agrees. Investigating the cases will help the community avoid imposing a blanket rule that may not take into consideration individual family situations. Perhaps some of the foreign wives have already turned to Israel's God and renounced their foreign gods. Only those who have not or are unwilling to do so will be affected by the ruling.[12] It takes about three months for the clan leaders to investigate all the cases, after which actions are taken as previously decided (vv. 16–18).

Modern readers may find these actions rather harsh, but there are good reasons for them. **God's law has to be obeyed; there can be no compromising of Israel's faith through intermarriage with those who hold onto pagan religions.**

In contrast, the apostle Paul, while urging Christians not to marry unbelievers (following the general principle in 2 Corinthians 6:14 and 1 Corinthians 7:39), adds that those who are already married to unbelievers before they became Christian are not to divorce their spouses, for reasons mentioned in 1 Corinthians 7:12–17.

Why do Ezra and Paul seem to differ in their pastoral solutions? Further reflection may help us to understand. Ezra was dealing with the Jewish community, who were to retain their

religious purity as the nation that would produce the Messiah. He was dealing with Jews who were already under the law and who should have known better than to marry across faiths. Paul, however, was dealing with people who were converting to the Christian faith and who may have already been married to non-Christians.

[11] Kidner, *Ezra and Nehemiah*, 71.
[12] David Guzik, "Commentary on Ezra 10:16–17", 2006, https://enduringword.com/bible-commentary/ezra-10/.

Do you agree with the actions taken by the leaders? What are the disadvantages of taking immediate action without proper investigation? On the other hand, what if the investigation was postponed indefinitely?

What principles could be applied in the church today? Why is it important for us to confess and renounce sin?

Read Ezra 10:16–44

Have you been at a school assembly when errant students are asked to stand on stage while the principal scolds them publicly for their misbehaviour? It is an unpleasant experience, not only for those being reprimanded but also for the many others watching. In today's reading, we see a similar experience. This third list of people in the book of Ezra is a roll of dishonour, an offenders' list. All those guilty of having married foreign wives and who have to divorce them are listed. There are 17 priests, 10 Levites and temple workers, and 84 others, making a total of 111.

Heading the list are descendants of the revered high priest Joshua son of Jozadak (Ezra 10:18–19), who was co-leader with Zerubbabel (Ezra 2:2, 5:2; Haggai 1:1, 2:4), from the first group of exiles to return to Jerusalem. Joshua was part of the generation that built the temple, and had himself led in the building of the altar and supervised the construction of the temple (Ezra 3:2, 9). One would have expected his immediate descendants to have led exemplary lives, but sadly, they did not.

To be a son or descendant of an illustrious man of God is not a guarantee of holiness.

Just look at the wicked sons of Eli the high priest (1 Samuel 2:12–17), the corrupt sons of the prophet Samuel (1 Samuel 8:3), and the apostate grandson of Moses (Judges 18:30). These guilty descendants of Joshua promise to divorce their foreign wives and offer guilt offerings to seek God's forgiveness and make peace with Him (Ezra 10:19). It has been observed that while priests made up 10 per cent of the returnees, here, they make up 15 per cent of the cases. As Bible commentator Derek Kidner observes, the priests are no better than the rest.[13]

The total number of offenders who have to divorce their foreign wives is a tiny fraction of the total population, which might lead us to wonder whether the fuss has been much ado about nothing. However, the reaction of Ezra and the leaders, and the strong measures they take, underline how sin cannot go unchallenged in God's community; think of Achan in the Old Testament (Joshua 7) and Ananias and Sapphira (Acts 5:1–11). The book of Ezra ends on a rather sad note, emphasising Ezra's efforts as a reformer. He will reappear in the book of Nehemiah.

Some lessons to consider: First, it is important for Christians to pass on their faith in Christ to the next generation. Every generation must learn to have faith in God and relate with Him directly; God has children but no grandchildren. Second, sin is a serious matter and must be dealt with, both in the individual and in the church.

[13] Kidner, *Ezra and Nehemiah*, 72.

In what specific ways can you pass on your Christian faith, insights, and experience to the next generation?

Why is it important to deal decisively with sin in the church (see 1 Corinthians 5)? What did Jesus teach about exercising discipline in the church (Matthew 18:15–17; Titus 3:10–11)?

Read Nehemiah 1:1–4

God mobilises workmen to do His will at just the right time. We have already seen how God used men like Zerubbabel, Haggai, Zechariah, and Ezra. Now, God is going to use a man who serves in the royal Persian city of Susa: Nehemiah.

Nehemiah is the royal cupbearer, someone who supervises the king's food and drink to guard against poisoning attempts. He is a Jew who has remained in Babylon to serve the king. Now, he receives his call from God through news from Jerusalem, brought to him by his brother Hanani (Nehemiah 1:2).

That Nehemiah is a devout Jew who is deeply concerned about the welfare of his people in Jerusalem is clear in the way he closely questions his brother. The words he hears, like "great trouble", "disgrace", "broken down", and "burned", break his heart as they describe the sad condition of Jerusalem and her people (v. 3). More than 90 years have passed since the first group of exiles returned from Babylon to the holy city, but the general situation there is not good. Although the temple has been rebuilt, the walls and gates are still in ruins, and the city lies exposed to enemies.

The news greatly troubles Nehemiah, who fasts and prays to God (v. 4).

His response is that of a man who knows that the real solution has to come from heaven—hence the prayer to "the God of heaven" (v. 4). His sitting down (rather than rushing into action), weeping, and praying expresses dependence on God, our true Helper (Psalm 54:4; Hebrews 13:6).

Today's passage shows us that the honour of God and His people must be important to us. The glory of God should be our central concern and motive. In the news we hear—about other individuals or families, the church, and what is going on in the world—we may hear God speaking to us and calling us to serve Him.

ThinkThrough

The news about Jerusalem affects Nehemiah deeply. How can we make reading the news more than an act of information gathering? Read today's news and see if God is saying something to you.

What situations facing those you know, your church, and society affect you deeply? What are you doing about them?

Day 30

Read Nehemiah 1:5–11

I knew an old missionary professor who could be talking to people one moment, then seamlessly break into prayer the next to talk to God, with his eyes open, about the matter that had just been shared. Indeed, God is the third person in any conversation, and today's passage teaches us that prayer should be our first action in all situations. Nehemiah's priority of prayer is the secret of his walk with God and his effectiveness in service. We must learn to turn information into intercession, and problems into prayer.

We can learn how to pray by looking closely at the various parts of Nehemiah's prayer. The acronym ACTS is sometimes used to teach Christians to include adoration, confession, thanksgiving, and supplication in our prayers. Nehemiah's prayer reflects similar content.

First, he focuses on the character of God, which is why we pray. He addresses his prayer to the "God of heaven" and the "great and awesome God" (Nehemiah 1:5), a phrase found in the Book of the Law (Deuteronomy 7:21, 10:17) and Psalms (Psalms 47:2, 66:3, 68:35). Nehemiah's knowledge of God is soundly based on Scripture and is the foundation of his prayer life. Note that the phrase "great and awesome" is repeated several times in the book of Nehemiah (4:14, 9:32).

Nehemiah also knows that God's eyes and ears are on His people (1:6; Psalm 34:17), hence his confidence in praying.

Second, confession is an important part of the prayer. Nehemiah's confession is both personal and collective (Nehemiah 1:6–7). Knowledge of God and ourselves is essential in prayer.

Third, the prayer emphasises the covenant between God and His people. Nehemiah reminds God of His special relationship with Israel and His promises to help the repentant Jewish exiles (vv. 8–9; see Deuteronomy 4:30–31; 30:4–5).

It is on the basis of God's character, Nehemiah's confession, and the covenant between God and His people, that Nehemiah makes a specific request: "Give your servant success today by granting him favour in the presence of this man" (Nehemiah 1:11). Do we sometimes jump too quickly to asking God for things without considering the basis of prayer? **In our prayers, do we reflect on who God is, our true spiritual condition, and our relationship with Him?** Nehemiah's prayer teaches us the priority and basis of all prayers.

ThinkThrough

What lessons can you learn about the importance of knowing God, yourself, and others, and remembering God's promises? What else does Nehemiah's prayer teach you?

Make a list of God's character and promises. Keep it next to your list of prayer requests. Reflect on how these two lists are connected. Then, pray.

Day 31

Read Nehemiah 2:1–5

Evangelist Billy Graham once observed, "To get nations back on their feet, we must first get down on our knees." Nehemiah knows this secret, so he prays day and night for four months. As he does this, a plan begins to form in his mind: he will approach the king about going to Jerusalem to help build its walls.

Nehemiah knows full well that the king's servants risk losing their lives if they appear sad before him (Nehemiah 2:1). It would have been seen as disrespectful or suggesting that the servant was unhappy with the king—or even plotting against him. Despite this, Nehemiah chooses to reveal his true feelings. The king, being a discerning man, notices his sad face and asks him what is the matter. This is a dangerous moment for Nehemiah, as he reveals to his readers, "I was very much afraid" (v. 2). Earlier, Artaxerxes, after hearing the Jews' enemies accuse the Jews of rebellion, had ordered the rebuilding work in Jerusalem to stop (Ezra 4:11–23).

Without mentioning Jerusalem, Nehemiah opens his heart to the king and reveals his grief over the condition of the city of his fathers (Nehemiah 2:3). Sensing that his cupbearer has a request, the king asks him, "What is it you want?" (v. 4). Nehemiah must have taken a deep breath—but not just to calm himself psychologically. He takes the opportunity to pray an "arrow prayer"—a quick, short prayer—even as he talks to the king. "Then I prayed to the God of heaven, and I answered the king" (vv. 4–5).

Nehemiah then makes his courageous request: he asks the king for permission to be sent to Jerusalem to help rebuild it (v. 5). This is a potentially explosive situation—how will the king respond?

We can apply two practical truths from today's reading. First, we must appreciate the importance of prayer and see its relationship with planning for personal action. **Pray, plan, then personally participate—this is Nehemiah's order of action.** We get into problems when we get the order mixed up. At all times, we must devote ourselves to prayer, for it connects us to God (Colossians 4:2).

Second, the answer to our prayers may be our own participation and may involve taking risks. As we pray continuously, we trust God to lead us (see 1 Thessalonians 5:17). Prayer warriors and godly risk takers often belong to the same tribe.

ThinkThrough

What do you think
of the order: Pray,
plan, and personally
participate? What
could happen if we
get the order wrong
or miss one of the
components?

Why is risk involved
in following and
serving God? What
fears keep you from
"making the most of
every opportunity"
(Ephesians 5:16)?
How does prayer
help?

Day 32

Read Nehemiah 2:6–10

Nehemiah is relieved to hear the king's positive response. The queen is present, indicating that this might have been a private, more relaxed setting, not a formal court session. Perhaps this helped soften the king's response. The king asks how long Nehemiah will be away in Jerusalem (Nehemiah 2:6). Nehemiah's answer is not recorded here, but we know that he will spend 12 years in the city (5:14; 13:6). The king sends Nehemiah (2:6), perhaps seeing that it is better to have an orderly and peaceful city than a rebellious and chaotic one, and knowing Nehemiah's loyalty and integrity.

Nehemiah then makes further requests. He asks the king for a letter to the governors of the Trans-Euphrates to ensure safe passage. In addition, the king sends a military escort to protect Nehemiah and his group (v. 9). Nehemiah also asks for a letter to the keeper of the king's forest so that he can secure adequate material for the work in Jerusalem. Timber is needed for repairing the wall and doors as well as for Nehemiah's house. Nehemiah has keen foresight: knowing he will be in the city for a long while, he plans ahead. Like Ezra, he knows that "the gracious hand of my God was on me" (v. 8; see Ezra 7:28). He knows that God is behind the king's favourable responses. As Christian author John

White notes, "No official can say no when God is saying yes."[14]

Nevertheless, Satan is also keenly involved in what is going on. We are briefly introduced to two characters who will create much trouble for Nehemiah and the people of Jerusalem. Sanballat the Horonite and Tobiah the Ammonite, leaders in neighbouring Samaria, are "very much disturbed that someone had come to promote the welfare of the Israelites" (v. 10). It is in their interest to have a weak and ineffective Jerusalem as their neighbour. They are instruments in Satan's hand to cause constant irritation to God's people.

Some people lack the faith to make bold requests when it is appropriate. Nehemiah, however, is not one of them. **Once he made up his mind about what God was asking him to do, he went about turning his vision into practical reality.** William Carey, the father of modern missions, said, "Expect great things from God; attempt great things for God." What he said was based on his deep faith in God, and God used him mightily. We may not be a Nehemiah or a Carey, but we can apply the same principles in our lives.

[14] John White, *Excellence in Leadership: The Pattern of Nehemiah* (Leicester: Inter-Varsity Press, 1986), 34.

ThinkThrough

What lessons can we learn from the way Nehemiah approached the king and made his requests? Is it true that "no official can say no when God is saying yes"?

Nehemiah had keen foresight, as evidenced in his requests. What is the relationship between faith and foresight? What happens when they are disconnected?

Day 33

It is often helpful to first examine a problem and see what needs to be done, quietly and prayerfully in the presence of God, rather than under the glare of the public spotlight. This is what Nehemiah does when he arrives in Jerusalem after a 1,000-mile-long journey. Like Ezra before him, he rests for three days (Nehemiah 2:11; Ezra 8:32); we can be sure he spends the time praying. Then, he embarks on a secret night inspection of the damaged walls and gates. **Nehemiah knows that it would be foolish to make a grand announcement and cause a stir without knowing in detail what needs to be done.** So, he wisely makes a private assessment of the damage to the walls first.

The inspection begins at the Valley Gate in the west, probably the easiest gate to get through. The Hebrew word for "examining" (Nehemiah 2:13, 15) means "careful probing", the way a doctor would examine his patient. Nehemiah probably inspects the walls with tears in his eyes, as he realises the severity of the damage and the vulnerability of the city's inhabitants. He goes along the wall southwards to the Jackal Well and the Dung Gate (v. 13) at the southern tip of the city. Then he proceeds northwards to the Fountain Gate and the King's Pool (v. 14). Nehemiah is unable to proceed further as there is too much debris for his horse to manoeuvre through. He seems to have dismounted to see more on foot, and then mounted his horse again to retrace his steps back to the Valley Gate.

Up to this time, Nehemiah had been keeping his plans to himself. "I had not told anyone what my God had put in my heart to do for Jerusalem" (v. 12). Now that he has seen enough to know how bad the damage is, how much rebuilding work is needed, and how huge and challenging the task will be, he is ready to speak to the local leadership.

Nehemiah's actions show us that clear, cool-headed and realistic assessment is needed before embarking on any task. Inner prayerful reflection in God's presence must precede public announcement and mobilisation. It is good to avoid showmanship and grandiose speeches that lead nowhere. "Think before you speak", "pray before you act", "know the problem well before you offer solutions", are good reminders that can apply in many situations.

ThinkThrough

Why is it important to examine a problem carefully in God's presence before doing something about it publicly? How can we avoid the temptation of making grand statements publicly before we have done so?

How do you think the other leaders might have responded when they realised that Nehemiah, though a newcomer, knew the situation very well?

Day 34

Read Nehemiah 2:17–20

Nehemiah's able and inspiring leadership is shown in the way he rallies the people. First, he points them to the *mess* they are in (Nehemiah 2:17), something they are aware of but do not know how to resolve. We must note that Nehemiah does not give the impression that he is an important visitor who has come to Jerusalem to fix their problem. He uses the pronoun "us" when describing the trouble they are in, indicating that he stands in solidarity with the people.

Second, he *mobilises* the people: "Let us rebuild the wall of Jerusalem" (v. 17).

Third, he describes the *method* they will employ to do the work: they are to work together in a united and coordinated way. His use of the plural "us" indicates that this is a work for everyone to be involved in.

Fourth, Nehemiah provides *motivation* for the work. He tells them that when they have completed the rebuilding work, God's city "will no longer be in disgrace" (v. 17). Jerusalem is the brunt of jokes among the surrounding people, and the honour of God is at stake. This is enough motivation for those who love God and revere His name to roll up their sleeves and get moving.

Fifth, Nehemiah reminds them that God is the Master Builder behind the whole thing; this rebuilding project is neither his own idea nor based on the strategy of the people. He gives his testimony of how God has led him and placed His gracious hand on him (v. 18). This is God's work and God is with His people. Such inspiring words would have helped to remove all doubts from the people's hearts and to encourage them to join hands in the work. They thus reply to Nehemiah, "Let us start rebuilding" (v. 18).

As the Jews begin their work, they encounter immediate opposition and ridicule from Sanballat, Tobiah, and Geshem, leaders of Judea's neighbours. Mocking them, "What is this you are doing?" (v. 19), these enemies contrast "this" and "you", and laugh at the perceived mismatch. They also accuse the Jews of rebelling against the king, which is a lie since the king has authorised the rebuilding work. Undaunted, Nehemiah replies that the work is God's, the people are God's servants, and God will give them success (v. 20). As Romans 8:31 also puts it, "If God is for us, who can be against us?"

Nehemiah is a godly mobiliser and motivator. He does not lord over the people, but works together with them. We motivate others when we roll up our sleeves to work with them. **The greatest motivation is the glory of God, when we can point others to the fact that what we are doing is for the name of the Lord, and that He is with us and leading us in the work.** Because God initiates His work and enables us to accomplish it, we should resist all temptations of offers by God's enemies to assist us. Satan will use them to disrupt the work. Moreover, anything done without faith is not pleasing to the Lord (Romans 14:23; Hebrews 11:6).

What would be the right motive for doing God's work? What lesser motives take away the joy and effectiveness of serving God?

Nehemiah refused to allow God's enemies to have any share in the work (Nehemiah 2:20). What principle can we apply based on this, in our personal lives and in the church?

Day 35

Read Nehemiah 3:1

Billy Graham wrote, "The purpose of this Christian society called 'the church' is first to glorify God by our worship." His words underline the central importance of worship. Nehemiah knew this too.

The rebuilding work begins with the repair of the Sheep Gate and the adjoining wall. Why does Nehemiah choose to start here? And why is the work done by Eliashib the high priest and his fellow priests (Nehemiah 3:1)?

The Sheep Gate, located at the northern tip of the wall, is closest to the temple. Its name came about probably because sheep were brought through it to be slaughtered as sacrifices in the temple. The gate's state of disrepair affects the worship of God, as commanded by the law. For this reason, its repair is a priority, which is why the high priest and his priestly team are personally involved. It is also the reason why, after the work is completed, the Sheep Gate and its nearby wall are dedicated (v. 1).

It must have been a high note in the building project. The repaired Sheep Gate encourages the Jews; like a flag planted in enemy territory, it serves as a rallying symbol that inspires soldiers to keep fighting during battle. The work on the wall then flows on from the Sheep Gate, all around the length of the wall, and back to the Sheep Gate.

Repairing the Sheep Gate first shows us how important it is to set our priorities right and keep our focus. The heart of life in Jerusalem is the worship of God. By repairing the Sheep Gate first, Nehemiah and his team are setting the tone for the entire work. They are stating that their first priority is the worship of God.

This is a lesson for us as well: our worship of God has to remain in sight all through the work we do for Him. It must never be lost in the details, no matter how complex or daunting the planning and coordination becomes. Truly, let us never neglect the worship of the Lord in our personal and corporate life. What is the point of rebuilding aspects of our life when our worship of God remains in ruins? How we worship God will determine how we serve Him.

What are common distractions that can diminish our worship of God?

How can we ensure that sincere worship of God remains at the heart of all that we are and do? Why is this of utmost importance?

Day 36

Read Nehemiah 3:2–5

The work that we do for God seldom goes smoothly. Unforeseen circumstances or opposition from adversaries can present formidable obstacles. Sometimes, problems may arise from within.

The rebuilding project has had a great start, with the Sheep Gate repaired, and work is now starting on the adjoining sections of the wall and gates. All is going well, with a section of the wall being repaired by the men from Tekoa. Then a problem emerges: the Tekoan nobles "would not put their shoulders to the work under their supervisors" (Nehemiah 3:5). These men stand out like a sore thumb among all the willing workers toiling together.

The Hebrew text in verse 5 is literally translated: "Their nobles put not their necks to the work of their LORD" (KJV). The basic problem is a refusal to submit, both to the Lord and to Nehemiah. Perhaps the nobles from Tekoa do not accept Nehemiah's leadership and plans, seeing him as an upstart who has only recently arrived in Jerusalem, whereas they have been providing local leadership for a long time. **Those who have become entrenched in positions of power, privilege, and authority sometimes refuse to welcome a new leader as they feel jealous or threatened, and will either not cooperate or even lead in opposition against such a leader.** The lesson here is this: humility and the willingness to work together with new or emerging leaders is necessary for the healthy functioning of the Christian community.

It is also possible that the Tekoan nobles consider it beneath their dignity to soil their hands in manual labour. That is the work of ordinary people, not of nobles. Yet, in exhibiting such an attitude, they show that they are less than noble. Jesus would say a few hundred years later: "Whoever wants to become great among you must be your servant, and whoever wants to be first must be slave of all" (Mark 10:43–44).

Tekoa is a town in the northern part of Israel. It had produced a great prophet—Amos—some 300 years before Nehemiah's time, but he was not from the ranks of the nobles. He was a simple shepherd whose heart was in tune with God (Amos 1:1). It appears that the nobles are made of different stuff. Thankfully, the bad attitude of the nobles of Tekoa does not dampen the work that is going on around the wall. Nor does it affect the attitude of the other workers, including the ordinary men from Tekoa, who, in addition to repairing their section of the wall, go on to repair another section (Nehemiah 3:27)!

Jesus declared that He came to serve rather than to be served (Matthew 20:28). He expects His followers to have the same attitude and to practise servant leadership (vv. 26-27), which He demonstrated by washing His disciples' dusty feet (John 13:1-17). Jesus has set an example for us to follow, and the ordinary Tekoan men are far better examples of this spirit of servant leadership than their leaders are.

Contrast the different attitudes of the Tekoan nobles and the other men. How can we avoid developing negative attitudes that impede the work of God?

How should we handle bad attitudes in the teams or groups we are a part of? When can those who refuse to cooperate take away the attention and appreciation we should show to the others in the team?

Read Nehemiah 3:6–32

The poor attitude of the Tekoan nobles is not mentioned again. However, today's reading emphasises Nehemiah's great leadership abilities to mobilise all to get involved in the work.

Everyone, including the chief priest and his fellow priests (Nehemiah 3:1, 28), works on the building project. The use of neighbourhood groups, identified by the repeated phrase "beside his house" or "each in front of his own house" (vv. 23, 28), and of existing family or clan groupings as well as professional groups (vv. 8, 32) to mobilise the people shows wisdom. If every neighbourhood takes care of the section of wall connected with it, it will not take much persuasion or effort to complete the project. **Nehemiah's organisational attention ensures there is no unnecessary overlap or neglected gaps in the work on the wall.**

The whole of Nehemiah 3 is filled with the words "rebuilt" and "repaired": this was "a time to build" (Ecclesiastes 3:3), a time to join hands in the work of God. The whole chapter rings with the sounds of construction work. About 50 people and their groups are mentioned in a continuous litany of "repaired . . . repaired . . . repaired". The Hebrew word for repair, *chazaq*, is used 35 times in Nehemiah 3; it means "to make firm or strong".[15]

This reminds us of the idea of edification that we find in the New Testament. Paul urges the church to be edified or "built up" (Ephesians 4:12), with the word for edification (*oikodomē*) suggesting the strengthening and constructive effects of sound teaching.[16] There is a continuing work of edification and repair to be done in our hearts and churches.

[15] Kidner, *Ezra and Nehemiah*, 87.
[16] W. E. Vine, *Expository Dictionary of New Testament Words* (Grand Rapids: Zondervan, 1952), 156.

ThinkThrough

Meditate on your role in God's work in your local church, and how your church fits into the larger work of God in the nation and in the world. How can you strengthen your participation in God's work?

What is the "repair work" that needs to be done in your life? Consider how sound teaching of the Word strengthens and edifies (see Ephesians 2:19–22). Pray that this will be so in your local church.

Day 38

Read Nehemiah 4:1–3

When we carry out God's work, we can expect difficulties and discouragement; Satan is never happy when God is obeyed and His work done.

As Nehemiah and the Jews rebuild the walls, they encounter Satan's attacks as Sanballat the Horonite and Tobiah the Ammonite, leaders in neighbouring Samaria, make disparaging comments to discourage the builders. This is intensive psychological warfare. As he sees the steady progress of the work, Sanballat "became angry" and is "greatly incensed" (Nehemiah 4:1). He starts mocking the Jews within earshot of his friends and the army of Samaria (v. 2), as he wants the others to join him in his mocking game—the more the merrier. He is aiming to cause maximum distress by increasing the volume of his taunts.

Sanballat asks a number of sarcastic questions designed to erode the determination of the Jews: "What are those feeble Jews doing? Will they restore their wall? Will they offer sacrifices? Will they finish in a day? Can they bring the stones back to life from those heaps of rubble—burned as they are?" (v. 2). He expresses doubt that they, being weak, will ever succeed in the building project that they have undertaken, for it is complex and massive. He suggests that even if the Jews appeal to God by offering sacrifices, they will not be able to restore the wall.

Tobiah, Sanballat's sidekick, joins in with a joke about the quality of the work of the Jews. He says, "What they are building—even a fox climbing up on it would break down their wall of stones!" (v. 3). Archaeological findings, however, show that Nehemiah's wall was about nine feet thick, a formidable wall indeed.[17] Tobiah's snide remarks are as flimsy as the wall he claims Nehemiah is building.

The relentless onslaught of such insulting words can shake the confidence of even the bravest and strongest of us. It can be deeply discouraging and painful. **We need to develop the ability to recognise the difference between feedback from friends who care for us, and hostile criticism from those whose aim is to dissuade and discourage us.** If we are not able to discern the difference, we may end up ignoring friendly feedback when it is actually meant to help us improve and prevent mistakes. Or, we may get so worked up by the critical words of those who are against us that we fall prey to their tactics and give up the work that God has called us to do.

[17] Jonathan Lamb, *Faith in the Face of Danger: An Introduction to the Book of Nehemiah* (Milton Keynes: Keswick Ministries and Authentic Media, 2004), 60.

What is the difference between friendly feedback (Proverbs 27:6) and adversarial criticism (Matthew 12:24; 2 Corinthians 10:10)? How should we respond to these?

Christians may be mocked by those who wish to attack their faith. What are some examples of this? How should Christians handle such attacks?

Day 39

Read Nehemiah 4:4–9

When we are insulted and mocked, what should we do?

Nehemiah could have tried to engage his opponents and debate with them as to why the building project would succeed. He knows well, however, that this would be a waste of time. It would not change their hearts or their destructive plans. Instead, he chooses an exemplary response—he prays. As one who knows God personally, he speaks into His ear, "Hear us, our God . . ." (Nehemiah 4:4). There is no attempt to speak into the ears of men (whether Persian king, Jewish leader, or potential ally), for it is enough to let God know the situation.

Nehemiah is grieved that the people of God are despised (v. 4). When God's people are mocked, it means God is mocked. What Nehemiah prays next (vv. 4–5) has to be read in the context of how imprecatory psalms (e.g., Psalms 83 and 137) are understood. Here, words that may seem harsh or vindictive are used against the enemies to express how those who love God feel when He is insulted. They are born out of a deep sensitivity towards God's honour and justice.

The sentiments Nehemiah expresses in his prayer are never acted out; rather, he leaves the matter to God to deal with. Such sentiments of moral outrage against evil are not incompatible with Jesus' command to love and pray for our enemies (Matthew 5:44). The Lord Jesus condemned His opponents as "snakes" and a "brood of vipers" (Matthew 23:33), but He also prayed for the forgiveness of His persecutors (Luke 23:34). If we understand this, then we will understand Nehemiah's prayer.

Nehemiah refuses to be sidetracked or distracted by the scathing insults of Sanballat and Tobiah. He prays, hands the problem over to God, then continues the work God has given him. As he writes: "So we rebuilt the wall till all of it reached half its height" (Nehemiah 4:6). He also notes that the people "worked with all their heart", putting in their best efforts. The more the enemy insults them, the more determinedly the people work. **The enemy's taunts only serve to fan the flames in their hearts for doing God's work.**

We need God's wisdom to handle unfair or even hostile criticism. There is a time for engaging in dialogue to create better understanding. But there is also a time for staying focused on the work God gives us, so as to avoid being distracted

How can Satan attack us and make us lose our focus? Why is praying to God and leaving the opposition in His hands almost always the best policy?

by meaningless or unproductive argument. We can bring all situations to God in prayer, asking for discernment. We should avoid taking insults personally and becoming emotional in our reactions. Remember that Satan is often behind hurtful and insulting words.

How can we pray against evil and yet pray for the salvation of those who cause us trouble? Reflect on how we can follow Jesus' example in this.

Day 40

Read Nehemiah 4:10–15

Aperson may be able to ignore insulting words, but the threat of violence is an entirely different matter. Furious that the work on the wall is progressing well, the enemies of the Jews—Arabs, Ammonites and Ashdodites—plot to "come and fight against Jerusalem" (Nehemiah 4:7–8).

Thus far, the Jews have responded well to the taunts of their enemies, but the imminent threat of violence makes some of them worry. Such negativism is often infectious, and soon, Nehemiah begins to hear excuses from within the ranks of his workers: "The strength of the labourers is giving out, and there is so much rubble that we cannot rebuild the wall" (v. 10).

Discouragement is creeping in. The people are looking more at the rubble that has to be cleared rather than at the wall that needs to be rebuilt. **They are looking at themselves more than at God who strengthens them.** The Jews are beginning to believe the enemy propaganda spreading among them, that they will be easily attacked and killed (vv. 11–12). They are listening to enemy voices more than God's Word or the words of their godly leader. This same attitude can often be seen in our spiritual lives. No one enjoys clearing rubbish and debris, but we have to clear what Bible teacher J. I. Packer calls "attitudinal rubble" such as "laziness, unbelief, procrastination, cynicism, self-absorption, in-fighting and fence-sitting" if we want to make spiritual progress.[18]

To allay their fears, Nehemiah leads the people to do the right thing: pray to God (v. 9). He also takes defensive action, posting family groups to guard vulnerable spots along the wall (v. 13). He then inspects the defences and gives a rousing speech to assure the people that God is with them, exhorting them to stand together to defend Jerusalem (v. 14). He then notes with satisfaction, "we all returned to the wall, each to our own work" (v. 15). Threats of violence cannot turn a man away from his God or his mission if he has such faith and resilience.

Today, most of us are spared the threat of physical violence arising from our faith in Christ. Sadly, however, there are places in the world where such dangers are a regular occurrence faced by the followers of Christ. It is important to remember these brothers and sisters in prayer. We may also find ourselves in similar situations if we are serving God in hostile places. Even if there is no threat of physical violence, we may face other kinds of overt or subtle persecution, which can deeply discourage us. At such times, we must seek comfort and refuge in the God who calls us and who is with us.

[18] J. I. Packer, *A Passion for Faithfulness: Wisdom from the Book of Nehemiah* (London: Hodder & Stoughton, 1995), 108.

The threat of violence made some of the Jews hesitate in their work for God. What would it take for you to stop doing God's work?

Nehemiah took practical steps to defend the people and the work, but carried on God's work. What lessons can we learn from him on how we should handle threats and danger?

Day 41

Read Nehemiah 4:16–23

In today's reading, we delve further into the details of Nehemiah's defensive measures. Realising that there is a spiritual battle going on, Nehemiah takes measures to ensure the work on the wall can proceed uninterrupted. He organises the workers into work teams and armed groups. Half will work while the other half will guard the city with armour and weapons (Nehemiah 4:16), with their military officers standing behind them to protect them.

The sight of armed guards and officers will help the workers concentrate on their work and do it without fear. Those who carry materials may have had to walk outside the wall, and would have been particularly vulnerable. So they are instructed to carry the building materials "with one hand and held a weapon in the other" (v. 17). Those who work on the wall have to use both their hands for their work, so they each "wore his sword at his side as he worked" (v. 18).

Moreover, Nehemiah has a trumpet blower with him all the time, so that he can rally the people even though they are spread out. If any part of the wall is attacked, the trumpet blower will sound the alarm and gather defenders to ward off the attack (vv. 19–20).

At the same time, Nehemiah reminds the leaders that even with all these military strategies, they must not forget that it is indeed "Our God" who "will fight for us!" (v. 20). The defensive army of Jerusalem is effective only because God is with them. Ultimately, the battle belongs to God (1 Samuel 17:47; 2 Chronicles 20:15).

"So we continued the work," Nehemiah observes with satisfaction (Nehemiah 4:21), having effectively converted the people into "guards by night and as workers by day" (v. 22). The people do not let down their guard even when they rest at night. The work on the wall, and the honour of God, is too much at stake. Nehemiah sets a personal example of this attitude. He shares, "Neither I nor my brothers nor my men nor the guards with me took off our clothes; each had his weapon, even when he went for water" (v. 23). They are never off duty.

There are spiritual lessons for us here. As we live for and serve Christ, we will realise that we are in a spiritual battle, in which Satan is working with the sinful world and fallen human nature to thwart our growth in Christ and our work for Him. **Just as Nehemiah and his people took appropriate** defensive measures, we too must be spiritually watchful and alert (Matthew 25:13; 1 Peter 5:8). We must encourage one another in this spiritual battle, as some may feel they are more in the line of fire than others. We must stand together in faith and courage.

Read Ephesians 6:10–18. How does this passage help us to apply the principles found in Nehemiah 4:16–23 in our spiritual lives? How are your spiritual defences?

How can we balance between focusing on defensive measures and doing the work of God? Are there any changes that need to be made in your life in this regard?

Day 42

Read Nehemiah 5:1–5

A good general who is leading his troops against a strong enemy would know that winning the battle is not just a matter of weapons and military tactics; it also depends on the morale and unity of the men. It is difficult to win a battle when soldiers are quarrelling among themselves or when there is a lack of discipline.

Nehemiah faces a similar challenge. Not all is well within the community in Judea. The poor have fallen victim to hard times and oppressive conditions. They raise a "great outcry" (*tsa`aqah*) against their better-off Jewish brothers and sisters (Nehemiah 5:1). The Hebrew word *tsa`aqah* is the same one used to describe the reactions of the Israelites when they were suffering under the oppressive whips of their Egyptian masters. God had heard their outcry and sent Moses to lead them out of Egypt (Exodus 3:7, 9). We can learn more about the present conditions of the poor in Jerusalem by looking carefully at what they say.

First, some are saying, "We and our sons and daughters are numerous; in order for us to eat and stay alive, we must get grain" (Nehemiah 5:2). Because all the men are at work on the wall, many are not working at their normal jobs to feed their families. The women thus have difficulty feeding themselves and their children. Such needs have been apparently overlooked, and some are in desperate situations.

Second, some say, "We are mortgaging our fields, our vineyards and our homes to get grain during the famine" (v. 3). The famine has made matters worse. The poor have run out of resources and have no choice but to mortgage their properties to buy food, which in famine conditions must have become relatively expensive.

Third, some find themselves in an even more desperate situation. They have had to sell their children into temporary slavery because what they get from mortgaging their property is not enough for their needs (v. 5). Not only do they have to find money to pay for food, they also have to pay taxes imposed by the Persian king on their fields and vineyards. Cracks are appearing in the community even as the rebuilding project is progressing well.

This is often also true in the local church today. **It is possible that the church may be so task-oriented that community and personal needs are being neglected.** We live in a society that tends to be driven

by KPIs (key performance indicators) and the successful completion of tasks. If we imbibe such values uncritically in our family lives and church activities, we may end up with unhealthy families and congregations where people are struggling because we are driven by priorities that may not be God-directed. Even as we focus on tasks, we must pay attention to relationships.

Think of those in your workplace and church whose needs should be heard. What can you do to help?

It is possible that while tasks are pursued, the community may suffer. What community needs may get sidelined as the church becomes task-oriented? How should they be resolved?

Day 43

Read Nehemiah 5:6–11

One of the managers in a *Dilbert* comic strip asks: "Who's up for some leadership?" He then continues, "Watch me define behaviour, align your goals with company objectives, prioritize respect, deal directly with conflict, maintain a positive attitude, and pretend to care."

Whatever leadership involves, godly leaders always should care genuinely. Nehemiah is such a leader. When he hears about how the poor are suffering, he is "very angry" (Nehemiah 5:6). He does not react defensively, giving excuses that it is inevitable that such a massive project would produce hardship. Instead, he "took counsel with myself" (Nehemiah 5:7 ESV), pondering prayerfully on what he hears. He then turns his anger into constructive action and begins to take steps to set things right. Here is passion and wisdom working hand in hand. Accusing the nobles and officials of breaking the law by charging interest for loans to their own people (v. 7), he calls for a town meeting.

At the gathering, Nehemiah accuses the wealthier Jews of making slaves of their poorer neighbours and robbing them of their dignity and freedom (v. 8). Jew is not to enslave Jew, yet this shameful thing is happening. Nehemiah demands that they stop charging interest if they fear God (v. 9), while also admitting that he, too, is lending the poor money and food (v. 10). The charging of interest is prohibited as God forbids profiteering (Leviticus 25:35–37). (Note that the biblical prohibition is directed at those seeking to make money from the poor, not necessarily at those doing business deals with others with means.)

Calling for true compassion and generosity, Nehemiah goes beyond what is legally required. He tells the leaders to return to the poor the interest they have charged and the properties that have been mortgaged, so that the poor would have a chance to recover from their dire circumstances (Nehemiah 5:11). These principles of the Jubilee are enshrined in the Law (Leviticus 25:8–55), and have to be followed if the people are to function as a God-fearing, just, and compassionate community.

Righteousness has to do with right relationships (with God and others). It is possible that we may think we are right with God—not realising that we are not because we are not treating others rightly. "Anyone who does not do what is right is not God's child, nor is anyone who does not love their brother and sister"

(1 John 3:10). James, too, speaks against favouritism and discrimination against the poor, which makes the church hypocritical and affects its relationship with God. As individual Christians and churches, we must ensure that our righteousness is directed not only to God but also to others around us.

Bible scholar Alec Motyer said that hypocritical Christians are "praying on their knees on Sunday and preying on their neighbours on Monday."[19] How true is this, and how can we live out our faith daily and practically?

How would you explain the biblical teaching on charging interest and the implications for Christians today? How can we avoid exploiting the poor directly and indirectly?

[19] Cited in Lamb, *Faith in the Face of Danger*, 44.

Read Nehemiah 5:12–19

The congregation is like a body. Any deformity or malfunction must be set right and not left to grow more serious.

Nehemiah is keen to restore the spiritual health of the community. His speech makes a powerful impact, for the people immediately agree to set things right in their community, giving the poor an opportunity to recover (Nehemiah 5:12). Making the priests, nobles, and leaders take an oath before the living God, Nehemiah warns those who are not intending to take their promises seriously that they will suffer adverse consequences (vv. 12–13). When everyone ("the whole assembly") says "Amen" (which means "so shall it be") and praises the Lord (v. 13), this is a sweet moment of unity and obedience. The encouraging thing is that "the people did as they had promised" (v. 13). Their promises are not superficial.

In the rest of the passage, we get a better picture of Nehemiah's generosity and his relationship to God and his fellow Jews. Nehemiah testifies that during his 12 years as governor, "neither I nor my brothers ate the food allotted to the governor" (v. 14). The previous governors of Judah had taxed their subjects excessively, but Nehemiah is different, for he has "the fear of God" (v. 15 ESV). He does not abuse his position, and refuses to tax the people because he knows how much they are suffering because of the building project (v. 18). Instead, he pays for his personal needs out of his own pocket (see Acts 18:3; 1 Corinthians 9:1–15).

As governor, Nehemiah is expected to provide food for his staff and diplomatic visitors. At his table, 150 staff and visiting diplomats are fed (Nehemiah 5:17). In all of his personal needs and the official exercise of his governorship, Nehemiah acts with personal sacrifice (v. 18).

Nehemiah reveals one more fact about himself. His focus is the building of the wall, and everything is subsumed under that primary goal (v. 16). He does not do business or acquire land—something he could have easily done as governor—to build up his personal wealth. **He knows that God has not sent him to acquire land but to build the wall.** He is thus able to pray for God to remember him and his actions (v. 19), reiterating that all he does is for God, and that any reward he receives, he would expect from heaven rather than earth.

There are some lessons to learn here. First, there must be a sincere and strong desire to set things right when

How do you think
Nehemiah inspired
the people through
his personal exam-
ple? Think of people
you know who
exude generosity,
self-sacrifice, and
compassion. Pray
about how you can
do the same.

Nehemiah lived a
focused life. Read
Psalm 86:11 and
2 Timothy 2:4. Why
is an "undivided
heart" (Psalm 86:11)
necessary if we are
to walk closely with
God and serve Him
faithfully?

they are wrong, whether it is in our own walk with
God, our family life, or what we do in church. Spiritual
neglect has serious consequences. Second, we
must act on our desire to set things right, whether
it means avoiding sin, carrying out loving deeds,
or forgiving others. Third, we must remain focused
on our relationship with God and others, and in
serving Him for His glory. We have to learn to live
with an "undivided heart" (Psalm 86:11).

Day 45

Read Nehemiah 6:1–9

A good American football player needs determination to overcome opposition that will come from all sides. He has to deftly avoid opponent team players or skilfully push them away, and fight his way forward to score a touchdown.

So far, Nehemiah has had to deal with relentless opposition and he has persevered. The rebuilding work is almost complete; all that remains is to place the doors on the new gates (Nehemiah 6:1). Out of desperation, Sanballat, Tobiah, and their partners try a new trick: they send a diplomatic letter inviting Nehemiah to a meeting (v. 2). Such a letter may have seemed flattering to a lesser man, but Nehemiah is not enticed. He senses that the offer is insincere. It is a delaying technique, intended to destroy Nehemiah's reputation—if he accepts, what would people think about his previous insistence on being focused and not compromising with enemies? Nehemiah's reply shows where his heart is: "I am carrying on a great project and cannot go down. Why should the work stop while I leave it and go down to you?" (v. 3).

The enemies send the same invitation three more times, but each time, Nehemiah gives the same reply (v. 4); he does not waste time composing new responses. Then, they change tactics and send a fifth letter, unsealed so that the contents are made public (vv. 5–7). They say that rumours are circulating that Nehemiah and the Jews are plotting to revolt against the Persian king, and offer to help. The unsealed letter is meant to spread the fake news. It is intended to strike fear in Nehemiah's heart and force him to negotiate with them. This would destroy everything he has built.

Nehemiah, however, flatly denies all the insinuations (v. 8). Whether he feels any fear is not known to us. It is not whether we experience fear that is important, for fearlessness can also mean foolhardiness. **What is important is what we do with our fears.** Whatever the case may have been in Nehemiah's situation, he does something in keeping with his character and faith, something that is always helpful whether we feel fear or not—he prays (v. 9).

Writing about Satan's numerous tricks against God's people, the Puritan writer Thomas Brooks noted that we should not be discouraged because we have in the Bible "precious remedies against Satan's devices"[20]. Some of us may suffer Satan's attacks, which can be either openly hostile or subtle; this is often the case if we are in positions of spiritual leadership (including parents and Sunday school teachers) or if we are doing something important for the Lord. We must not be distracted or discouraged in such circumstances, but learn to keep our eyes on the Lord rather than on the traps of our spiritual opponents (see Psalm 141:8–9).

[20] Thomas Brooks, *Precious Remedies Against Satan's Devices* (Edinburgh: Banner of Truth, 1968).

How does it feel to be falsely accused? What are some common reactions? What lessons can we learn from Nehemiah's actions?

Nehemiah's prayer focused not on removing the difficult circumstances, but asked for strength to face them (Nehemiah 6:9, see also Acts 4:29). Does this shed light on how you can respond to a difficult situation you may be facing?

Read Nehemiah 6:10–14

Dealing with Satanic opposition from outside the church is difficult, but dealing with subtle opposition arising from within the church is worse. Shemaiah (probably a priest) invites Nehemiah to meet him at the temple, claiming that assassins are coming to kill Nehemiah at night. Shemaiah offers the temple as a safe place (Nehemiah 6:10). **Such a message would make anyone panic, especially if it came in the form of a religious prophecy.** But Nehemiah is unmoved for various reasons.

First, he discerns that Shemaiah is not sent by God (v. 12). Second, he recognises that Shemaiah is a traitor working for Tobiah and Sanballat (v. 12). Third, he knows his enemies are trying to intimidate him (v. 13).

Tobiah and Sanballat want Nehemiah to panic and hide inside the temple, going where only priests are allowed to go (Numbers 18:7). If he had followed Shemaiah's suggestion, he would have been guilty of disobeying God's law. Nehemiah must have known that in the history of Israel, King Uzziah—who was not a priest—had gone into the temple to burn incense in an area restricted only to priests, and God had instantly struck him with leprosy (2 Chronicles 26:16–20). Though

Nehemiah has no intention of offering incense, he is not willing to sin against God by entering an area prohibited to non-priests, even if his life is in danger (Nehemiah 6:13).

Nehemiah knows well the battle plan of the enemies (see 2 Corinthians 2:11). So he tells Shemaiah off, "Should a man like me run away? Or should someone like me go into the temple to save his life? I will not go!" (Nehemiah 6:11). Resolute as ever, he refuses to be hoodwinked.

True to form, Nehemiah again turns to God in prayer (v. 14). He prays for God to judge his enemies, who include opponents inside the walls of Jerusalem. Some of them are religious figures: Nehemiah mentions a prophetess and other prophets who are working in collusion with the enemies outside and have become their hirelings (v. 14). He is in an unenviable position, but God is with him.

There are some important lessons for all of us. First, we should remember that God's work must be done according to God's ways. Paul described the Christian disciple as an athlete who competes according to the rules (2 Timothy 2:5). Just as an athlete running a race would be disqualified if he broke the rules, so a Christian displeases the Lord when he tries to do God's work but not keep His rules, for example, by not being honest, fair, and kind. Our character and obedience are important to God. Second, wicked suggestions can come even from people we think are religious. We need to be prayerful and discerning in determining when a suggestion is pleasing to the Lord and when it is not.

What are common ways in which Christians may break God's rules even when doing God's work? How can we avoid this?

What thoughts and habits within us work in opposition to what God is doing in us? How do they work in collusion with the devil and the sinful world? What can we do about them?

Day 47

Read Nehemiah 6:15–19

One of the times when we have to be most vigilant against the tricks of the devil is immediately after a great victory. The prophet Elijah had a tremendous victory over the false prophets of Baal when God displayed His awesome power on Mount Carmel. But after this, Elijah suffered from fear, discouragement, and self-pity (1 Kings 18:16–19:9). Today's reading shows us potential vulnerability after a moment of victory.

It is amazing that in spite of the size and complexity of the project, the logistical challenges, the constant opposition from enemies, and the problems within the community, the building project is completed in a mere 52 days (Nehemiah 6:15)! The wall was 4 km long, about 12 m tall (the height of four storeys) and about 2.7 m thick. It is such an amazing feat that the enemies of the Jews and the surrounding nations who hear about it are afraid (v. 16). They realise that the powerful God of the Jews is with them, and wonder what else they are capable of.

Still, some of the enemies do not give up disturbing Nehemiah. Satan is the same; he will never rest until he is put out of the way. His aim is to disrupt, disturb, and denounce anything that has to do with God. After so great an accomplishment,

there is no immediate celebration. Instead, Nehemiah has to take action to ensure there is no further danger to the people of Jerusalem.

Letters are going back and forth between the nobles of Judah and Tobiah (v. 17), who has connections with some important people in the city. Tobiah has married into the family of Shekaniah, whose father had been one of the pioneers among the returning exiles (see Ezra 8:5), and has had his son marry into the family of Meshullam, one of the key builders of the wall (Nehemiah 6:18; 3:4, 30). These nobles and their clans are beholden to Tobiah; they are probably bound by trade deals and contracts.

The Jewish nobles "kept reporting" to Nehemiah Tobiah's "good deeds" (Nehemiah 6:19), propaganda that is intended to change Nehemiah's view of his enemy. They try to be peacemakers and intermediaries, carrying messages back and forth. On the surface, their actions appear praiseworthy. After all, the wall has been completed, and it is time to be reconciled and to carry on. But Nehemiah knows that they are playing into the hands of the scheming Tobiah. Aware of Tobiah's evil intentions, he notes, "Tobiah sent letters to intimidate me" (v. 19). If any of us think we are under heavy

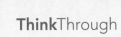

ThinkThrough

enemy fire, we should draw inspiration from Nehemiah.

Nehemiah did not have time to rest on his laurels and celebrate his victory. **The enemy attacked relentlessly, using subtle forms of temptation, which one can miss in the triumphant emotions after a victory.** Nehemiah teaches us how important it is to be vigilant and prayerful, especially after great achievements and victories in our lives. We are to be "alert and of sober mind" (1 Peter 5:8) because our enemy, the devil, has many subtle tricks to use against us.

What can we learn from Nehemiah about being alert and discerning?

How can well-meaning Christians be used by Satan to cause one to make ungodly compromises?

Day 48

Read Nehemiah 7:1–3

The enemies try every trick in their book to bring Nehemiah down, but the man remains resolute and close to God. He quietly and urgently takes appropriate action to secure the city, appointing gatekeepers and other residents (Nehemiah 7:1, 3) to stand guard.

It is important to guard what has been built with effort and sacrifice. If we merely focus on building but fail to take steps to guard what has been built, all our efforts may go to waste when the enemy enters to disrupt and destroy. We may have been given a new heart when we place our faith in Christ, but we must learn to guard it. "Above all else, guard your heart, for everything you do flows from it" (Proverbs 4:23). **How easily the enemy can influence our thoughts, attitudes, habits, and relationships through what we see, hear, or read.** How seriously we should be guarding our eyes and ears through which so much of the world enters us.

In taking steps to guard the city, Nehemiah appoints trustworthy leaders—his brother Hanani, who visited him in Susa, and Hananiah, the commander of the citadel. Hananiah is "a man of integrity" who "feared God more than most people do" (Nehemiah 7:2). These men have

good credentials and Nehemiah is wise to choose them. Nehemiah also gives instructions for the gates to be shut at night and to be reopened only when "the sun is hot" (v. 3). This is to prevent spies and other enemies from entering and leaving the city in the darkness, and other illegal and subversive activities. In posting many of the guards "near their own houses" (v. 3), Nehemiah exercises wisdom: a man would be extra vigilant near his own house as any breach of security would first affect his own family.

We have to guard what God has blessed us with: our personal walk with God, our families, our churches, and our service for the Lord. We do well to remember that "Unless the LORD watches over the city, the guards stand watch in vain" (Psalm 127:1).

It is easy to be complacent and allow the enemy to infiltrate our lives. The alarm system in an office or home is designed to go off when intruders try to gain illegal entry. In the same way, our regular habits of Bible reading and meditation, prayer, worship, reading good literature, being part of an accountability group, and acting according to a Christian conscience are ways in which we can develop a spiritual alarm system to warn us of possible infiltration by the evil one and his ideas. Above all, we must pray for the Lord's protection to "deliver us from the evil one" (Matthew 6:13).

What lessons can we learn from Nehemiah's actions to guard Jerusalem, and how can we ensure that our spiritual alarm system is working well? See 1 Corinthians 16:13.

Read Philippians 4:7. How does the peace of God guard our hearts and minds in Christ? How is such peace connected with prayer (v. 6) and thinking godly thoughts (v. 8)?

Day 49

Read Nehemiah 7:4–73

It is a common mistake to think that great ministry has only to do with such activities as preaching, singing, and putting up a great show on stage. People seldom think of those who quietly work behind the scenes, organising events, making lists, preparing itineraries and inventories, and keeping records. This is because such work is considered mundane, so attention is usually given to more visible and audible ministries.

This part of the book of Nehemiah (Nehemiah 7:4–73), along with other sections (3:1–32; 10:1–27; 11:1–12:47), contains administrative records. We tend to skip such sections, for they contain information that seems irrelevant to modern readers. Who is interested in census records or inventories (see Numbers 7)? Why are these rather laborious texts included in Scripture? What is God's intention of leaving these details in the Bible?

Among many possible reasons, such lists remind us of the importance given by God to those who work hard (administrators, scribes, secretaries) in keeping records. God himself is mentioned in the Bible as keeping records (Luke 10:20; Revelation 20:12). As governor, Nehemiah keeps good and detailed records. He is already thinking of how the population in Jerusalem can be increased and adequate housing can be provided

(Nehemiah 7:4). To do this, he has all the families registered, and in the process, finds the list of those who had returned 90 years earlier (v. 5).

Neatly set out in verses 6 to 69, this list is comparable to the one in Ezra 2:1–67. There are some differences, which may be due to updating— late arrivals and corrections—and possible scribal errors. The similarities, however, emphasise that the work begun by Sheshbazzar and the original group of exiles is now coming to completion in Nehemiah's day.

The records provide names and numbers; even the domestic animals are counted and recorded (Nehemiah 7:66–69). There is also a record of contributions to the building project (vv. 70–72). These carefully maintained lists suggest to us that Nehemiah is not only a visionary leader but also a diligent administrator. **He has the discipline of a record-keeper not simply because he is obsessively interested in records, but also because it helps him to lead and serve well.**

We must remember that the ability to administer well is a spiritual gift (see 1 Corinthians 12:28 ESV). The administrator who sorts out arrangements and takes care of finance and personnel is doing as significant work for the Lord as the preacher at the pulpit. The administrators in our churches and Christian organisations, who often work quietly behind the scenes, need to be encouraged and appreciated. How about sending them an encouraging message or telling them how much you appreciate their important ministry?

How can we know that God is keenly interested in every name on His lists (Psalm 56:8; Luke 12:7)? How does that encourage you? Take time to thank Him for how He cares for you personally.

Try making a few lists, e.g., people you are praying for or how you are spending your time. Such lists remind us of our blessings and responsibilities. What have you discovered from your lists?

Day 50

Read Nehemiah 8:1–9

Nehemiah 8 records a high point in the book, when the people gather with tangible unity to worship the Lord (Nehemiah 8:1). They ask Ezra to bring out the Law, which he does before the assembly (v. 2). **The reading and proclamation of God's Word should happen each time we gather to worship God, as it is an essential part of worship.** We note here three aspects of the centrality of God's Word in our lives.

First, it is relevant. Ezra reads the Word for six hours (v. 3), while a group of Levites explains what is written so that the people can understand (v. 8). The people listen carefully (v. 3); they are interested in the truth in God's Word and want to apply it in their lives. To understand God's Word is to see its relevance for daily living.

Second, we note the deep reverence for God's Word. When Ezra opens the Book of the Law, "the people all stood up" (v. 5). Reverence is shown not just by standing up, but even more importantly, by obeying God's Word. In other words, reverence for God's Word is shown by accepting its authority, cherishing it, and obeying it. We need to develop the psalmist's attitude to God's Word: "my heart trembles at your word" (Psalm 119:161); "I have put my hope in your word" (v. 81); "I keep your precepts with all my heart" (v. 69). We show our reverence for God's Word by obeying it not only individually but also as families and corporately as a church.

Third, the people respond to God's Word. When Ezra opens the Book and praises God, the people respond by saying "Amen! Amen!" (Nehemiah 8:6). They join Ezra in praising God, lifting their hands (which meant they prayed) and by bowing down with their faces to the ground and worshipping God (v. 6). This is the proper response to God's Word.

The people also weep when they hear the law (v. 9). God's Word comes as a spiritual sword that cuts deep into sinful and negligent hearts (Hebrews 4:12); it is depicted as a powerful hammer (Jeremiah 23:29) that can break stubborn hearts—not to destroy but to redeem and rebuild. And when it enters ears and lands on hearts, it can reprove and correct (2 Timothy 3:16). Weeping in response to God's Word has often been a sign of revival in the history of the church. How wonderful when God's Word moves the hearts of people.

Have you experienced the Bible's relevance for daily living, and how have you shown your reverence for it? Do you see areas where you need to deepen your experience?

How do people show that they have been deeply moved by God's Word? How can you pray for more of this in your church?

Day 51

Read Nehemiah 8:10–18

God's Word had a profound effect on the people who heard Paul's preaching in Thessalonica (1 Thessalonians 1). They welcomed the message, became a model congregation, and shared the gospel with others.

Something similar happens in Nehemiah's day. The people weep so much that Nehemiah, Ezra, and the Levites have to restrain them (Nehemiah 8:9–11). The people are told that it is a special day of the Lord, meant to be celebrated with joy. Would it have been better for the leaders to let the people fully express their grief? Counselling students are taught that one should not stop a person from crying, as it will short-circuit the process of catharsis and impede the ventilation of deeply held emotions. Are the leaders too quick to stop the weeping?

A fuller expression of grief in response to God's Word is envisaged, as we can see from Nehemiah 9. Thus the leaders are not cutting short what God is doing, but in wisdom, they are preparing the people for a deeper repentance later on, in the context of fasting and prayer. **The people accept the calming advice of their religious leaders and recognise that the day is meant to be spent in joyful worship and fellowship in honour of God who has assisted them.** So they enjoy meals together and compassionately share them with the less well-off, sending "some to those who have nothing prepared" (8:10, 12).

The people also obey what has been revealed to them—a commandment to "live in temporary shelters during the festival of the seventh month" (v. 14; Leviticus 23:33–43). This Feast of the Harvest (Exodus 23:16) is one of three annual festivals in Israel. It is to be celebrated with the first fruits of the harvest and is to be celebrated for seven days marked by restful joy. Its purpose, as expressed by God, is to remind His people that "I made the Israelites live in temporary shelters when I brought them out of Egypt" (Leviticus 23:43). The people are to remember that as sojourners and pilgrims, they continue to depend on the Lord to provide for their journey through the wilderness of the world.

The people take action to obey God's Word. Having long neglected the Feast, they now celebrate it with much joy (Nehemiah 8:17). Their joy is the joy of obedience. There is weeping, joy, sharing, and obedience—the proper kind of response to God's Word.

How do we respond when we read, meditate on, and hear the proclamation of God's Word? Is it a deep experience, producing in us a range of emotions and actions that show that God's Word is powerful as it richly dwells in us (Colossians 3:16) to stir our hearts and move our hands in obedient and compassionate actions?

What are the dangers of letting religious emotions expressed in public become uncontrolled? How would you assess the advice of the leaders in Nehemiah 8?

Reflect on how God's Word brings forth in us weeping, joy, sharing, and obedience. Assess how much of this is experienced in your personal reading of Scripture, as well as in church.

Day 52

Read Nehemiah 9:1–15

Church reformer John Calvin said that when we worship, we say something about God and something about ourselves. The latter is done through confession and repentance, which are important dimensions of true worship. We recognise these elements in this passage.

The Israelites' joyful celebration is followed by heartfelt confession of sins in a service of repentance led by the Levites (Nehemiah 9:1–5). The people gather to fast, "wearing sackcloth and putting dust on their heads" (v. 1)—a traditional way of expressing grief and repentance (Joshua 7:6; Job 2:12; Jonah 3:5). They "separated themselves from all foreigners" (Nehemiah 8:2), as that has led to them absorbing the idolatry of their pagan neighbours. This was what had led their forefathers to sin, which was ultimately why God had handed them over to foreign powers who took them into exile.

The reason for the separation from the surrounding world is to keep Israel faithful to God and holy like Him. Any interaction that could corrupt the nation is to be discarded. This, of course, doesn't mean that we should form a holy huddle and do away with all contact with the world—assuming this were actually possible. Separation from the world must always be seen together with the call to be a witness to the world (Mark 16:15; Genesis 12:2–3). Holiness and mission must always go together.

The service lasts six hours, with three hours spent reading the Book of the Law, and the rest of the time confessing and praising God (Nehemiah 9:3). In particular, they "confessed their sins and the sins of their ancestors" (v. 2). The simple order of service should be noted: first, the reading and exposition of God's Word; then, second, a response to God's Word through confession and praise. The weightage given to each of these components serves as a model for worship today.

The people then pray the longest prayer in the Bible (vv. 5–38). The prayer starts off with acknowledging God as the Creator and giver of life to all (vv. 5–6). He is the only true God who deserves all our worship. This great God revealed himself to Abraham and led him into the promised land (vv. 7–8). He made a covenant with His people and blessed them. He rescued them from Egypt and brought them again to the promised land (vv. 9–15). He gave them His law (vv. 13–14).

It is good to base all our prayers on the foundation of who God is, His relationship to us, and what He has done for us. Even our confessions to Him make sense only because of who He is. When we worship God, we focus on who God is (almighty, holy, loving, and merciful) and who we are (sinners in need of God's forgiveness, and helpless in an uncertain world). **The more we know God, the more we will know ourselves.** The result is high praise, deep confession, and sturdy trust in God.

Why are holiness and mission necessarily connected to one another? What happens when the two are disconnected? Consider how your life reflects both holiness and mission, and pray for any area that may need strengthening.

Why is our knowledge and trust in God the bedrock of all our prayers? How can we ensure that this is so? How is confession of sins deepened and made more real when we consider who God is?

Day 53

Read Nehemiah 9:16–37

The history of sin and the mystery of God's grace. This is what we find woven into the long prayer in Nehemiah 9:5–38. The Jews had been guilty of repeated sinful disobedience; they were spiritually deaf and "refused to listen" (vv. 16–17, 29). Suffering from spiritual amnesia, they kept forgetting what God had done for them and were ungrateful. They were also spiritually defiant, continuing in their sins against God (vv. 26, 35). They deserved God's just punishment, for they broke their covenant with God and turned against Him. The phrase "But they" appears several times (vv. 16, 26, 28, 29), standing as sad markers of Israel's continual apostasy and rebellion.

God, however, was repeatedly gracious. What is amazing is that for every "But they" there is a "But you" (vv. 17, 27, 28, 31). Every instance of turning to sin was met by a gracious response from God, who forgives His people and rescues them from dangerous situations. He does this because of His character: "You are a forgiving God, gracious and compassionate, slow to anger and abounding in love" (v. 17).

God does not abandon His people and "desert them" in the desert (v. 17). He acts with "great compassion" (v. 27) and "great mercy" (v. 31) because He is a "gracious and merciful God"

(v. 31). The Jews admit that in His dealings with His people, God has always "remained righteous" and "acted faithfully" even though His people have "acted wickedly" (v. 33). They have repaid God's kindness with more wickedness! Yet God has not given up on them and keeps the story going with His endless supply of grace.

Divine grace will outlast human sinning (see Romans 5:20; 1 Timothy 1:13–14). It was on this basis that the Jews tell God about their "great distress" (Nehemiah 9:37) and plead for Him to respond graciously one more time, just like He had responded so many times before. We know that Israel kept on sinning until the arrival of Jesus, who is God's answer to the problem of persistent sinning. Having died for our sins, Jesus offers us freedom from stubborn sinfulness and help in times of trouble.

There is no sin so deep from which God cannot redeem us, if we repent and turn to Him for mercy. Some people may find themselves in the deepest pit and think they are beyond redemption. The prodigal son, for example, found himself in the worst of circumstances. When he decided to repent and return to his father's house, however, he received his father's loving forgiveness and warm embrace (Luke 15:17–24).

God redeems us from the deepest pit (Psalm 103:4). If you know someone who feels trapped, you can share with them God's amazing grace, which can redeem people from the most terrible pit.

What are the signs that someone is suffering from spiritual deafness, forgetfulness, and defiance? What would be effective remedies for these conditions?

For the truly repentant, God's grace overcomes the worst forms of sins (Romans 5:20). But why should we not take God's grace for granted (Romans 6:1; Hebrews 10:26–31)?

Day 54

Read Nehemiah 9:38–10:31

The Israelites' prayer service of repentance ends with the making of a "binding agreement" (Nehemiah 9:38; "firm covenant", ESV). The usual Hebrew word for covenant is *berith*, but a different word, *amanah*, is used here, referring to a solemn pledge to remain faithful.

It is time to break the sordid cycle of sin that has marked the history of God's people. The heart of the covenant is a promise to be faithful to God. Put in writing and signed by the leaders with the support of all (10:1–29), the binding covenant carries the weight of serious intent, unanimity, and accountability. The people promise to be separate from the neighbouring peoples who were practising idolatry (v. 28), and also to carefully obey all the Lord's commands (v. 29). They also refer to God as "our Lord", reiterating a renewal of their identity (v. 29). Separation (holiness) and obedience are to be the marks of their new faithfulness.

While the Israelites promise to observe all of God's law, they highlight three areas that need special attention. First, they promise not to engage in intermarriage, which has been a lingering problem (v. 30; see Ezra 9, 10). Second, they commit themselves to observe the Sabbath (Nehemiah 10:31; Exodus 20:8–11), which had been broken by rampant commerce. Third, they promise to give their tithes faithfully so that the house of God will not be neglected (Nehemiah 10:32–39).

The emphasis on marriage, the Sabbath, and tithes covers key areas of life: the family, the marketplace, and the community of God. Discipleship must be taught holistically, and faithfulness to God must be seen in each of these key spheres.

Today, family life is threatened by many harmful trends and influences, and must therefore be guarded. There are increasing signs of dysfunctional family relationships, and families are exposed to worldly values and habits that can become forms of idolatry and addiction. These must also be resisted.

The observance of Sabbath, as applied today, gives importance to God, our worship of Him, and rest.

But our busy routines today rob us of rest and worship, devotion and reflection. The church and the kingdom of God should be of paramount importance to us.

Why is it important
to make it a point
to obey God and
seek holiness?
How are these
often neglected in
individual Christians
and churches? What
can be done to
strengthen them?

How can the pursuit
of holiness and the
commitment to
obey God be lived
out in the family,
marketplace, and
the church?

Day 55

Read Nehemiah 10:32–39

A boy receives two coins from his father, one to drop into the offering bag in church and the other for ice-cream after service. On his way to church, he plays with one of the coins, tossing it and catching it in mid-air. Then he misses, and the coin falls into a drain. Unable to retrieve the coin, he looks up and says, "Sorry, God, there goes your coin!"

What is our attitude to the giving of tithes and offerings? The longest section of the Israelites' covenant has to do with the matter of giving so that the public worship of God can flourish (Nehemiah 10:32–39). The people promise to tithe from their crops to the Levites (v. 37) in return for their service to the Lord (Numbers 18:21). On their part, the Levites are to contribute a tithe from the tithes they receive (Nehemiah 10:38); this portion is called "the LORD's offering" (Numbers 18:26). **The people vow to ensure that the priests and Levites are adequately taken care of so that they can continue serving the Lord and the community in leading in the worship of God.** Unlike the other tribes, the tribe of Levi, from which priests and Levites come, have no agricultural land of their own.

In addition, the people also promise to give a third of a shekel annually for the service of the house of the Lord (Nehemiah 10:32). Though not stipulated in law, it is a kind of temple tax that will enable worship at the temple to continue. The money will be used to buy regular offerings and "for all the duties of the house of our God" (v. 33). Mention is also made of how wood for the altar is to be supplied (v. 34), and the people also promise to bring to the temple the firstfruits of their farms and families as thanksgiving and dedication (v. 37).

These details may seem remote to us, because for Christians today there is no temple, Levites, and priests, and many of us live in urban environments, not agricultural ones. However, the principles are still applicable, as we have churches, mission agencies, pastors, missionaries, and church workers who require financial support. We do not have temple taxes, but should we be expected to tithe? Some churches note that the practice of tithing (as defined in the Old Testament, see Leviticus 27:30–33) is still applicable today, but others point out that the New Testament standard of giving is not so arithmetically precise (which might lead to a form of legalism), but encourages generous and self-sacrificial giving instead. What is given must be given willingly, cheerfully, and sincerely (2 Corinthians 8:1–7). Those who give their time to serve the Lord must be supported (1 Timothy 5:17–18) so that God's work is not impeded by lack of funds.

Why are New Testament standards of Christian giving higher than compulsory tithing? In what ways is Jesus watching how we give (Mark 12:41–44), and why is this important? Assess your own giving to the Lord.

The Lord Jesus taught that "the worker deserves his wages" (Luke 10:7). Is there any ministry or worker that you know of who may need your help?

Read Nehemiah 11:1–12:26

In keeping with their commitments to tithing, the Israelites decide to increase the number of residents in Jerusalem, which is currently on the low side. While the leaders have settled in the city, Jerusalem needs a sufficient number of residents in order to be viable economically and to be secure.

It is understandable that many prefer to live on their own farms and lands. That way, they can provide for their own needs, without the problems associated with earning a living in an urban setting. In addition, it may have been considered safer to live outside a city with a long history of being attacked by invaders.

Whatever the reason, it is determined that one out of every ten residents outside Jerusalem will be brought into the city to live. This is decided by casting lots (Nehemiah 11:1). Apparently there is also a sense of voluntarism in all of this, as "the people commended all who volunteered to live in Jerusalem" (v. 2); it could be that those selected did not complain and went willingly to live in Jerusalem, and were thus appreciated for their sacrifice and commitment.

The rest of chapter 11 records (with Nehemiah's typical administrative efficiency) the names of the heads of families of priests, Levites, and other Jews who live in Jerusalem. The gatekeepers are also mentioned (v. 19), as are those living in the surrounding villages and other towns (vv. 25–35). Chapter 12 contains a list of priests and Levites who came with the earlier groups. Nehemiah keeps these records not just for reasons of proper administration and order, but also as a record for posterity. He is both an excellent administrator and archivist.

This part of the book ends on a happy note. **Everybody is settled in their home, worship in the house of the Lord is adequately provided for, and Jerusalem is secure from enemies.** The implications for us today are twofold. First, we need many people to serve in church and para-church organisations. Second, Jerusalem was underpopulated then, but today, God's kingdom is found all over the world, and more workers are needed in God's great vineyard, the mission fields. Will more Christians volunteer sacrificially to go, live, and serve in these places? Each of us must seek to serve in some way in church (there are always things to do if we ask those in charge) and participate in mission work by going, praying, or supporting missionaries.

If your church were to challenge her members for full-time service, how many workers would be mobilised? Is God calling you to be one of them?

All Christians are called to serve the Lord in their "secular" jobs and activities. How can you apply this to your own life and work?

Day 57

Read Nehemiah 12:27–47

Today, we come to another high point in the narrative: it is time for the dedication service for the completed wall of Jerusalem (Nehemiah 12:27). Joy permeates the account. The Levites enter the city to "celebrate joyfully" (v. 27), the worshippers "offered great sacrifices, rejoicing because God had given them great joy" (v. 43), and the women and children express joy, so much so that "the sound of rejoicing in Jerusalem could be heard far away" (v. 43). When something is completed for the glory of God, especially after encountering and overcoming numerous setbacks and obstacles, it is time for joyful celebration.

Two large choirs walk on top of the wall in opposite directions till they meet at the Gate of the Guard, then they go into the temple. One choir is led by Ezra and the other by Nehemiah (vv. 31–40). It is likely that Nehemiah is actually leading the second choir, though he humbly describes himself as *following* the choir (v. 38).

A purification rite is also carried out. The priest and Levites purify themselves first, likely with the blood of sacrificed animals. Then they purify the people before purifying the wall (v. 30). This is reminiscent of how the priests, the furniture and vessels used in the tabernacle, and later the temple, were purified (Exodus 40:1–16). We should note that the dedication of a wall or building is insufficient if the people are not similarly dedicated. It is a good practice in similar dedication services of church or ministry-related buildings to first have the people dedicate themselves by committing themselves to the Lord. **Without the dedication of hearts, the dedication of brick and mortar is of no value.**

The joyful celebration at the dedication of the wall continues with an account of how everything is in place in the proper functioning of the temple in Jerusalem (Nehemiah 12:44–47). The workers in the temple—priests, Levites, and singers—are able to perform their service for God because all that is needed is provided for by the people. The system of contributions for the temple services and for those who serve in the temple is in place, and things seem to be going smoothly. Daily provisions for singers and gatekeepers are provided and the portions to support the Levites and priests are not held back (v. 47).

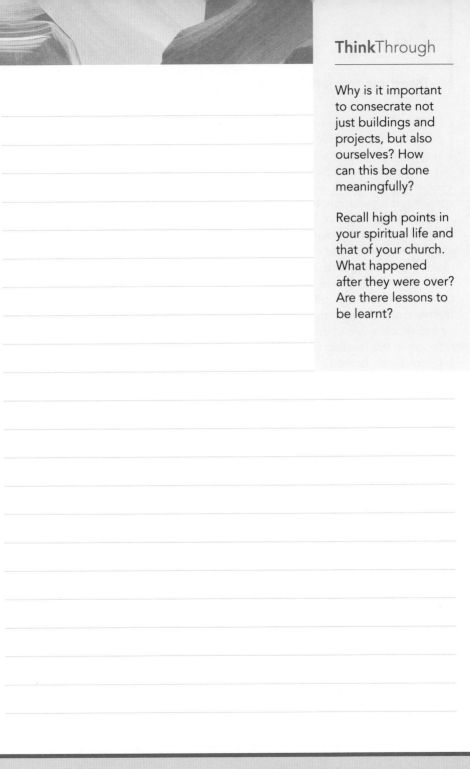

Why is it important
to consecrate not
just buildings and
projects, but also
ourselves? How
can this be done
meaningfully?

Recall high points in
your spiritual life and
that of your church.
What happened
after they were over?
Are there lessons to
be learnt?

Read Nehemiah 13:1–14

It hurts when people break their promises. In today's reading, we see that Nehemiah is in for some big disappointments. Seeing that everything is in order, and having completed his mission, Nehemiah returns to his old job in Susa (Nehemiah 13:6). Scholars believe he stayed there for a year or more before making another trip to Jerusalem (v. 7). He is in for a rude shock. When he arrives, he finds out, much to his frustration and anger, that the very points that the Jews had promised to observe in the binding covenant have been blatantly broken.

First, the promised tithes have reduced to a miserable trickle (v. 10). The storerooms in the temple are meant for the tithes given by the people and materials for the worship of God, but sadly, Eliashib the high priest, who is in charge of the storerooms, has let his friend Tobiah use a large room (v. 7).

Tobiah, being a layman and a foreigner, has no right to be in the temple. It is sacrilegious for him to occupy "a room in the courts of the house of God" (v. 7). How could Eliashib, who should have known better, allow this? How could Tobiah, who had mocked God and His people, be allowed to stay in God's holy temple? By letting him stay there, Eliashib has done an "evil thing" (v. 7). We are also told that the high priest is "closely associated with Tobiah" (v. 4). If God's servant makes an evil alliance with God's enemies, he will soon be used by them to bring dishonour to God's name.

Nehemiah is "greatly displeased" and evicts Tobiah (v. 8). He then has the storerooms purified, because the presence of Tobiah and his possessions have desecrated them. After this, he orders the rooms to be filled with "the equipment of the house of God" (v. 9).

Eliashib had allowed Tobiah to occupy the large room because it was empty. And it was empty because the people had neglected to bring their tithes and offerings into the temple. As a result, the Levites did not receive their support and had to go out into the fields to earn their income (v. 10). The priests also suffered as a result. **These are the consequences of the people's disobedience, adversely affecting the worship of God in the temple.** Nehemiah rebukes the leaders for breaking their promise to not neglect the house of God (v. 11; see 10:39). He then appoints trustworthy men to be in charge of the temple storerooms and ensures that the flow of tithes is restored (13:12–13).

How can spiritual enemies gain entry into our hearts and churches? How can they affect our walk with God, and our worship and service?

We are the temple of the Holy Spirit (1 Corinthians 3:16; 6:19). How can we detect the enemy's presence in this temple? What should we do if we find this to be so?

The implication here for us is that we have to be careful that spiritual enemies do not set up camp in and among us. It can happen subtly and imperceptibly. Regular Scripture reading and prayerful self-examination will help us to be on our guard.

Read Nehemiah 13:15–22

Another major lapse that Nehemiah discovers among the people when he returns from Susa is their blatant disregard of the weekly Sabbath.

The Israelites had promised that they would observe the Sabbath diligently, but now, work is being done on the Sabbath and a roaring trade is going on (Nehemiah 13:15–16). The gates of the city are left wide open for traders selling produce from nearby farms and from as far away as Tyre, where fish caught in the Mediterranean Sea are brought in. The Sabbath is being desecrated, God's law is being broken (see Exodus 20:8), and the nobles do not seem to care. They have shirked their duties.

For Nehemiah, this is a serious matter. It calls for urgent action. Nehemiah does not shrink from doing what is necessary, no matter how difficult, unpopular, or unpleasant it is. He calls the nobles and rebukes them, reminding them that it is because their forefathers had done the same thing that calamity had befallen the nation and the city in the past (Nehemiah 13:17–18). In repeating the sins of their ancestors, they are "stirring up more wrath against Israel by desecrating the Sabbath" (v. 18). **Nehemiah then takes the necessary measures to ensure that the Sabbath will be kept.** He orders the gates of Jerusalem to be shut tight throughout the Sabbath (v. 19). Not simply trusting mechanical solutions, he also places men he can trust at the gates to make doubly sure that no merchandise enters the city (v. 19).

Testing his resolve, the "merchants and sellers of all kinds of goods spent the night outside Jerusalem" (v. 20). This happens a few times. We can imagine the merchants calling out their wares hoping that the gates will open for business to continue. But Nehemiah remains unmoved. He sternly warns the merchants that he would arrest them if they persist (v. 21). They must have felt the razor-sharp edge of his words because "From that time on they no longer came on the Sabbath" (v. 21). Nehemiah also takes further precautions by posting Levites to guard the gates. There is to be no compromise when it comes to obeying God's law.

We live in a fast-paced society. Demanding workplaces and a distracting world of entertainment tend to take away precious time necessary to attend to our relationships with God and loved ones. God's Sabbath rule—that we must rest adequately every week (Exodus 20:8–11)—is necessary for our spiritual, physical and emotional health. We must not become so busy that we ruin our well-being in these important areas.

Read Deuteronomy 5:13–15. Why did God establish the Sabbath law? How can we apply Sabbath principles to how we worship God, find time to rest, and spend time building relationships?

How can greed and the relentless pursuit of wealth, fame, and entertainment rob us of our restfulness in Christ? Read Matthew 11:28–30. How can you find rest in Christ as a regular experience?

Day 60

Read Nehemiah 13:23–31

The Israelites had made a covenant to cease the practice of intermarriages with idol-worshipping neighbours. But they continued to marry women from the neighbouring states of Ashdod, Ammon, and Moab (Nehemiah 13:23), which may lead them to embrace idol-worship.

An additional serious consequence has to do with their children, half of whom speak the foreign languages of their mothers and "did not know how to speak the language of Judah" (v. 24). Hebrew is being lost as the mother tongue in Judah, and this would have grave repercussions. These children would not be able to read the Hebrew Scriptures nor participate in the Hebrew liturgies of worship, which is a prescription for the loss of faith among the next generation. This leads us to wonder whether similar processes are at work today, not only through religiously mixed marriages, but also by our failure to teach the young gospel truths and a biblical vocabulary, which can result in them embracing the languages and thought patterns of the ungodly world. The corruption of the next generation and their "paganisation"[21] poses serious challenges to the church.

Again, Nehemiah has to rebuke the guilty parties. Angry at their stubbornness, he "called curses down on them" and "beat some of the men and pulled out their hair" (v. 25). The beating is probably part of a formal punishment (see Deuteronomy 25:1–3). Pulling out hair (which might refer to the shaving of the head as a penalty) is reminiscent of what Ezra did with his own hair (Ezra 9:3).[22] Nehemiah makes the Jews take an oath that they will cease intermarriages with foreigners who do not share their faith (Nehemiah 13:25), citing the example of King Solomon who married foreigners and was led into sin (v. 26). The practice of intermarriage, he makes clear, is a "terrible wickedness" and is "being unfaithful to our God" (v. 27).

The problem has infected the highest places. One of the grandsons of the high priest Eliashib, the man who had kicked off the building of the wall, has married the daughter of Sanballat, Nehemiah's old nemesis. Nehemiah is so upset that he "drove him away" (v. 28). Such priests had "defiled the priestly office" and the covenant it represented (v. 29). Nehemiah then has the priests and Levites purified from all foreign influences (v. 30).

What lessons can we learn here? First, we need to be aware of how our beliefs, values, principles, and

How can we avoid being corrupted by ungodly people while still interacting with them and reaching out to them with the gospel?

How can we ensure that we speak the language of the Christian faith and teach the same to the next generation?

habits can become corrupted as we interact daily with the world and its ways. We cannot avoid these interactions, but we can avoid their negative impact by remaining faithful to the Lord Jesus.

The letters that the risen Christ sent to the seven churches in Asia Minor in the book of Revelation (Revelation 2–3) remind us that we can lose our original love for Christ, fall prey to heresy, and compromise on holy living. We need to guard not only our lives and families, but also our churches. The Lord has enabled us to remain faithful, and we can seek to trust and obey Him as we await His return to establish His kingdom forever.

[21] Kidner, *Ezra and Nehemiah*, 131.
[22] Packer, *A Passion for Faithfulness*, 193.

Journey Through
Ecclesiastes

by Philip Satterthwaite

Ecclesiastes is one of the five Old Testament wisdom books. Unlike the rest of wisdom literature however, Ecclesiastes seems to present us with more questions than answers, more contradictions than agreements! But Ecclesiastes is worth wrestling with. As the Teacher takes us through the different approaches to life, we are struck with the question: How, then, should we live? How should we regard work and pleasure, justice and politics? Take a journey through Ecclesiastes to discover how we should live life "under the sun" as a faithful disciple of Christ.

Dr Philip Satterthwaite has been a Lecturer in Old Testament and Biblical Hebrew at the Biblical Graduate School Of Theology in Singapore since 1998, and was its principal from 2011 to 2019. His main research areas are in the Old Testament's historical and wisdom books, and he has authored several books.

Journey Through
Psalms 1-50
by Mike Raiter

It's often called the songbook of the Bible, with its many beautiful and inspiring songs of praise, thanksgiving, and lament. But the book of Psalms is much more. It is also a proclamation of trust in God's goodness, a remembrance of His deliverance, and a pledge to godly living. And it points forward to the ultimate expression of that goodness and deliverance—Jesus. Start on a journey through Psalms 1–50, and rediscover why we can rejoice, weep, and put our hope in our Shepherd, Judge, and King.

Journey Through
Proverbs
by David Cook

The book of Proverbs is much, much more than a poetic collection of pithy, common-sense sayings. Dig deep into the teachings of Solomon, Agur, Lemuel, and others, and you'll be surprised by what you can learn from these men of ancient wisdom. You'll discover why true wisdom begins with "the fear of the Lord", how a relationship of reverence and love for God will lead to true knowledge, and how contemporary and relevant the book of Proverbs continues to be for life today.

Journey Through

Hosea

by David Gibb

As God's spokesman, Hosea is told by Him to marry Gomer, a prostitute, and to go again and again to woo her back despite her many infidelities. Hosea's commitment to love Gomer gives us a glimpse of God's love for us. God loves His people as passionately and as jealously as a devoted husband loves his wife. Even when we wander from Him and our hearts cool towards Him, He continues to come after us and to draw us back to Him. God's love will never let us go. Rekindle your love and commitment to the One who loves you!

David Gibb is the former Vicar of St. Andrew's Church in Leyland and Honorary Canon of Blackburn Cathedral. He is committed to training church planters and gospel workers, and is one of the contributors to a new NIV Study Bible. He is also author of a book on Revelation.

Thirsting for more?

Check out **journeythrough.org**

- **Find titles available**
- **Explore other formats:**
Read online or receive daily email

For information on our resources, visit **ourdailybread.org**. Alternatively, please contact the office nearest you from the list below, or go to **ourdailybread.org/locations** for the complete list of offices.

BELARUS
Our Daily Bread Ministries
PO Box 82, Minsk, Belarus 220107
belarus@odb.org • (375-17) 2854657; (375-29) 9168799

GERMANY
Our Daily Bread Ministries e.V.
Schulstraße 42, 79540 Lörrach
deutsch@odb.org • +49 (0) 7621 9511135

IRELAND
Our Daily Bread Ministries
64 Baggot Street Lower, Dublin 2, D02 XC62
ireland@odb.org • +353 (0) 1676 7315

RUSSIA
MISSION Our Daily Bread
PO Box "Our Daily Bread",
str.Vokzalnaya 2, Smolensk, Russia 214961
russia@odb.org • 8(4812)660849; +7(951)7028049

UKRAINE
Christian Mission Our Daily Bread
PO Box 533, Kiev, Ukraine 01004
ukraine@odb.org • +380964407374; +380632112446

UNITED KINGDOM (Europe Regional Office)
Our Daily Bread Ministries
PO Box 1, Millhead, Carnforth, LA5 9ES
europe@odb.org • +44 (0)15395 64149

ourdailybread.org